SOULS FOR SALE

Reel Spirituality Monograph Series

SERIES DESCRIPTION

The Reel Spirituality Monograph Series features a collection of theoretically precise yet readable essays on a diverse set of film-related topics, each of which makes a substantive contribution to the academic exploration of Theology and Film. The series consists of two kinds of works: 1) popular-level introductions to key concepts in and practical applications of the Theology and Film discipline, and 2) methodologically rigorous investigations of theologically significant films, film-makers, film genres, and topics in cinema studies. The first kind of monograph seeks to introduce the world of Theology and Film to a wider audience. The second seeks to expand the academic resources available to scholars and students of Theology and Film. In both cases, these essays explore the various ways in which "the cinema" (broadly understood to include the variety of audio-visual storytelling forms that continues to evolve along with emerging digital technologies) contributes to the overall shape and trajectory of the contemporary cultural imagination. The larger aim of producing both scholarly and popular-level monographs is to generate a number of resources for enthusiasts, undergraduate and graduate students, and scholars. As such, the Reel Spirituality Monograph Series ultimately exists to encourage the enthusiast to become a more thoughtful student of the cinema and the scholar to become a more passionate viewer.

SOULS FOR SALE

*Rupert Hughes
and the Novel Hollywood Religion*

TERRY LINDVALL

CASCADE *Books* · Eugene, Oregon

SOULS FOR SALE
Rupert Hughes and the Novel Hollywood Religion

Cascade Books
An Imprint of Wipf and Stock Publishers
199 W. 8th Ave., Suite 3
Eugene, OR 97401

www.wipfandstock.com

PAPERBACK ISBN: 978-1-7252-9306-9
HARDCOVER ISBN: 978-1-7252-9305-2
EBOOK ISBN: 978-1-7252-9307-6

Cataloguing-in-Publication data:

Names: Lindvall, Terry, author.

Title: Souls for sale : Rupert Hughes and the novel Hollywood religion. / by Terry Lindvall.

Description: Eugene, OR: Cascade Books, 2021 | Reel Spirituality Monograph Series | Includes bibliographical references.

Identifiers: ISBN 978-1-7252-8300-8 (paperback) | ISBN 978-1-7252-8299-5 (hardcover) | ISBN 978-1-7252-8301-5 (ebook)

Subjects: LCSH: Hughes, Rupert, 1872–1956. | Silent films—United States—History. | Religion in motion pictures. | Motion pictures—Religious aspects.

Classification: PN1995.9.R4 L56 2021 (print) | PN1995.9.R4 (ebook)

CONTENTS

Contents

ACKNOWLEDGMENTS

S tumbling on to this film brought together several of my interests, namely satire, Hollywood silent movies, and the Christian faith and tradition. Studying such a constellation of pleasures piqued my curiosity of the modernist trend of 1920s religion.

Various film scholars have contributed to this humble work. In particular, I would like to thank Tim Lussier of *Silents Are Golden* (http://www.silentsaregolden.com/) for his generosity in sharing images. To Fuller Seminary and its virile cinematic minds, Elijah Davidson, Kutter Callaway, and Rob Johnston, I am deeply indebted for their support and willingness to follow Chesterton's notion, that "if a thing is worth doing, it's worth doing badly." They have made this thing worth doing, but also made it much better. I thank copy editor Stephanie Hough for her keen eye and her astute skills in polishing my messiness and for doing so with such tact and grace.

I would thank my perspicacious colleague and remarkably enjoyable and brilliant friend, Craig Wansink, for making me his neighbor and allowing me to settle in his neighborhood, and for his incisive critical perspectives on my banal writing style. For their grand encouragement, my gratitude goes to the wonderfully recuperated Joe and Kathy Merlock Jackson. I thank my film encyclopedia

Acknowledgments

buddy, Dennis Bounds, who knows every quote ever said in any movie and can perform each with the right inflexion and accent. To my colleague and friend, Stu Minnis, who can capture a screenshot without blinking, thank you. To Ben Fraser, John Lawing, Bill Brown, Andrew Quicke, George Selig, and Gil Elvgren, all of whom have opinions and stories to go with everything, I am grateful.

For those quirky and motley saints who meet every Friday before dawn, Bobby Woodard, Hugh Patterson, Ben Unkle, Steve Scoper, Stuart Goldwag, Tim Robertson, Ben Fraser, Jock Freese, David Stewart, David Wilkins, Tom Klein, Robbie Berndt, Bob Tata and Andy Fox, thank you for your wit, wisdom, and prayers.

Thank you as well to Barbara Newington and Adelia "Dolly" Rasines for decades of encouragement and delight. I also owe enduring gratitude to Frank and Aimee Batten Jr. who will one day be judged for giving me the leisurely opportunity to research and write.

For the woman who has sought to keep me honest and happy for 37 years, and not failed to both reprove my soul and love me at every moment, Karen, I thank you. She has freely let me run off to Hollywood. For our kids, Chris (who writes comedy scripts with unbridled zest and wit) and Caroline (and her happy husband Cary), I grin and give them every penny I am making off this book, which will be only enough to buy one beer among the three of them.

INTRODUCTION

A simple comic scene in Mary Pickford's *Rebecca of Sunnybrook Farm* (dir. Marshall "Mickey" Neilan, Artcraft Pictures, 1917) subtly previews an impending change in early twentieth-century theology, as mediated by the growing community of Hollywood. Both a precursor and a portent, the parable portrays Rebecca being denied dinner because of her mischief. Her two austere aunts seek to discipline the irrepressible child by forcing her to clean up after their meal. As she tidies up, she discovers a tantalizing cherry pie that she must put away. Tempted to taste a slice, she pauses to look up and spies a sampler that reads, "Thou shalt not steal." She hurriedly releases her temptation and ruefully heads out of the kitchen. However, over the door of her exit hangs another sampler that promises: "God helps those who help themselves." She smiles, nods her assent, and hurries back to the pie, gobbling down the juicy dessert. For America's Sweetheart, and for a host of religious Americans who had endured a world war and an influenza epidemic, Benjamin Franklin's civil wisdom and common sense trump the commandment of the Decalogue. In the 1920s, American religion would enter its modern phase on the moving picture screen.

FIGURES 1–3

Mary Pickford chooses the American civil religion over the Decalogue's command not to steal in *Rebecca of Sunnybrook Farm* (dir. Marshall "Mickey" Neilan, Artcraft Pictures, 1917, courtesy Stu Minnis).

Historian Kristen Whissel investigated how moving pictures of the silent era helped "audiences make sense of, and find pleasure in, the experience of modern life." She explored how the technology of cinema helped to shape and define a modern sense of the national identity. An atheist author challenged this identity of the religious nation in the late decade of the twentieth century when he penned a subversive novel and then directed it as a motion picture to challenge the faithful with a vision of a dynamic new religion of Hollywood. Mass entertainment, rather than sermons and lectures, would dictate the creeds of the Jazz Age.

Introduction

One of the most popular Hollywood writers and directors of the early 1920s was Rupert Hughes, the uncle of eccentric billionaire Howard Hughes. Rupert dallied with women as much as his insatiable nephew would, marrying three times and regularly castigating marriage and divorce laws.[1] Hughes's book titles suggest some of his beliefs and practices: *The Lady Who Smoked Cigars*; *Ladies' Man*; *We Live but Once*; and *Souls for Sale*.

The publication of this last novel, *Souls for Sale*, sparked controversy over its satiric treatment of traditional Christianity. Appearing during the same era as the Modernist/Fundamentalist split at Princeton University, the work mocked what it saw as the hypocrisy of all forms of religious belief. However, while his book's fictional heroine felt the seductive allure to Hollywood, Hughes was equally dismissive of the film capital's own construction of illusory gods and goddesses. In 1921, he adapted this work for the screen, with a less inflammatory and more popular tone. But it still had its sting and would express the liberated zeitgeist of the Roaring Twenties and the emergence of the worship of the self. The film stands as a secular prophecy from an impish heretic, one that resonated with its times of flaming youth and secular ideals.

Hughes, notorious for his outspoken atheistic opinions, released *Souls for Sale* in 1922. Adapted from his own novel, the bowdlerized version of the film sought to subvert both the American religious culture and the emerging Hollywood dream machine. In an era in which Hollywood sought to clean up its public relations image, Hughes's work

1. Tragically, after his first wife divorced him in a scandalous trial, his subsequent two wives committed suicide. He lived with his third wife at the Ambassador Hotel, where his nephew Howard Hughes joined him and learned how to enjoy women in the notorious ways of Hollywood. See Longworth, *Seduction*.

mocked Middle America by playfully intimating that the new film capital has replaced the church as its most sacred place. His American heresy subverted the Midwestern Bible Belt in favor of the new heaven on earth, Hollywood, with its own saints, parables, and virtues.

Hughes's comic photoplay derided a prevailing fantasy that one could go to Hollywood and become a star overnight. The book and film established the enduring duality that the City of Angels was actually a city of demons, but one that offered a progressive secular religion in contrast to what he, like cynics Ambrose Bierce and Robert Ingersoll before him during the Golden Age of Freethinkers, viewed as the hypocrisy of the Christian nation. His texts conducted a sparkling tour of the holy land of movie land, while teasing spectators with glittering bits of bogus glamour, adventure, and romance. His films would even showcase some of the more glamorous celluloid saints, like Charlie Chaplin, before his Leta Grey scandal, and Mae Busch, with her bee-stung lips. Reassembled, stitched, cobbled together and restored by MGM and Turner Movie Classics for a 2006 screening, *Souls for Sale* offers a catalogue of thirty-five famous stars alongside its notable leads, an undisguised advertisement for Hollywood life and lifestyles of the rich and famous.

Yet Hollywood was not Hughes's only target. Church historiography offers a legitimate critique of how much American Christianity was becoming a consumer religion. In the 1920s, revivalists, including friends of Hollywood like Billy Sunday and Aimee Semple McPherson, self-consciously used modern media, entertainment, and celebrity to sell the faith.[2] They had been doing so for more

2. McPherson was the more controversial of the two, with an alleged affair with Milton Berle. In his memoir, Berle, *Milton Berle* (128–29), he notes that whenever he heard, "Yes Sir, That's My Baby,"

than a century and a half, going back at least to George Whitefield, the actor who became not only a trans-Atlantic revival preacher in the mid-eighteenth century, but a celebrity to people like Benjamin Franklin as well. Within public memory, the scandalous antics of the extremely popular Reverend Harry Ward Beecher with his trial over adultery added salacious fodder for Hughes's exposé.

Hughes's impish reputation flowered with this work. His early fame rested as much upon his musical compositions and upon what he saw as his "scholarly" research, where he demythologized heroes of American history like George "he did not cut down a cherry tree" Washington. Seeking to humanize the first president, his controversial biography attacked the legend of Washington's honesty and the fiction of his prayers and religious commitment. Although a fanatic patriot, having served in the military during both the Spanish American War and World War I, the press and public virulently attacked Hughes for such debunking. His art of mocking was just beginning, as he would enter the cultural battles between pious fiction and agnostic rejoinders with panache.

Situated in the early stages of Hollywood's later self-referential, meta-films (e.g., *Show People*, *The Bad and the Beautiful*, *The Big Picture*, *The Player*, etc.), *Souls for Sale* stands as a historical artifact that mischievously inaugurated a jaundiced celebration of the pagan culture, one which would be handled with more cynicism and irony in later productions. Hughes's film story of his heroine, Remember (aka "Mem"), can be read as a familiar narrative boilerplate that views religious people as self-righteous and out of touch and views the big city and film industry

---

he remembered her "in a very thin, pale blue negligee." She consulted with Charlie Chaplin on how to improve her public image; he once told her "Whether you like it or not, you're an actress."

as sleazy and corrupt. His tongue-in-cheek canonization of Hollywood as the new utopia began during the eruption of various movie scandals. Hughes thus positioned himself as a disturber of the peace who wanted to make waves as much as movies. *Souls for Sale* functioned as both an advertisement of what Hollywood could be and a prophecy of what it would become, all because of an impish heretic who wanted to preach his own myths.

However, cinematic representation of religion did not begin with Hughes. His writings erupted out of a pious tradition of evangelical literature, a religious embrace of the art of cinema, and western films that smacked of Presbyterian theology. Planted in the fertile soil of proselytizing and profiteering, Hughes produced fruit that would prove not only prophetic, but quite prickly for a pious public.

1

NINETEENTH-CENTURY EVANGELICAL FICTION AND MORAL PROPAGANDA

A heyday of religious publishing culminated near the end of the nineteenth century with the arrival of former New Mexico governor Lew Wallace's *Ben Hur* (Harper, 1880), subtitled *A Tale of the Christ*. Wallace had been aroused to the importance of religion after hearing the audacious and spellbinding rhetoric of the "great agnostic" Robert Ingersoll attacking belief in God and the divinity of Christ. In *The Gods and Other Lectures*, Ingersoll paraded his freethinking down Main Street, mocking the pious, "Banish me from Eden when you will, but first let me eat of the fruit of the tree of knowledge."[1] His cheeky excoriation provoked Wallace's indifference and ignorance of the Christian faith so much so that he resolved to investigate it closely, with the result of his own conversion and the publication of his famous novel.

---

1. Ingersoll, *Gods and Other Lectures*, cover. "It may be that ministers really think that their prayers do good and it may be that frogs imagine that their croaking brings spring."

The narrative sermons implanted in numerous religious novels also planted an expectation of God's communication being expressed in non-didactic and fictional forms. Back in 1872, Harriet Beecher Stowe, after writing her famous abolitionist novel, *Uncle Tom's Cabin* (claiming it was the result of divine dictation), called upon Christians to show forth their creativity:

> Hath any one in our day, as in St. Paul's, a psalm, a doctrine, a tongue, a revelation, an interpretation—forthwith he wraps it up in a serial story, and presents it to the public? Soon it will be necessary that every leading clergyman should embody in his theology a serial story, to be delivered from the pulpit Sunday after Sunday.[2]

Her summons inspired one "serial" preacher of note, Charles M. Sheldon. Borrowing the seed idea from British William T. Snead's *If Christ Came to Chicago?* (1894), Sheldon concocted a series of narrative sermons that were literary cliffhangers, blending evangelism and social work. Absolute ethical obedience and suffering stood as his litmus tests for following the Christian faith.

Following closely in 1896, Sheldon introduced the most enduring religious tract of the era, *In His Steps*, which asked the pesky, and much parodied, question, "What Would Jesus Do?" The book's tremendous popularity catapulted Sheldon onto the national stage where he would continue the inquiry into such areas as "What Would Jesus Do with the Drama?" Herein, the Lord gently castigated everyone concerned, from writers and producers to actors and exhibitors, for their greed, pandering, and lust. Ultimately, Jesus would set forth an ideal example of the participants working together for the uplift of all. In her dissertation,

2. Stowe, *My Wife and I*.

Susan Craig argued that the social gospel messages in books like Sheldon's shared common religious themes with silent films of the era. "Many, like those listed above, extol the virtues of study in advancing an enlightened faith, while celebrating the importance of direct contact simple human kindness (the 'Golden Rule') in dealings with the poor and outcast of society."[3]

On April 24, 1902, Sheldon published his views on "The Use and Abuse of Fiction" calling for works of art to "inspire the reader to higher and holier things."[4] His serial novel stemmed from Sunday evening sermons and it allegedly achieved for the "social gospel what *Uncle Tom's Cabin* did for slavery."[5] His book was the quintessential representation of an emerging genre of literature at the *fin de siecle*, the social gospel novel. Subsequently, visualized as a lanternslide picture play in early 1900, the book evolved into a silent film in 1916.

Sheldon's religious novel, however, inhabited a larger literary context, in which according to Brown University historian Carl F. Kaestle, "Dime novels, beginning in the 1860s, were the first highly profitable mass-market fiction, and Westerns were the predominant genre among the dimes."[6] In her examination of early evangelical writing, publishing, and reading, from the Methodist Book Concern in 1789 through the publication of works like Lew Wallace's *Ben Hur*, Cathy Gunther Brown found evangelicals appropriating narratives of purity and transformation from popular texts of sermons, Sunday school material, cheap tracts, hymns, and novels packaged for the faithful.

3. Craig, *Skin and Redemption*, 48.

4. Sheldon, "Use and Abuse of Fiction," 967.

5. Smith, "Charles M. Sheldon's *In His Steps*," 47.

6. Kaestle, "History of Readers," 33.

As readers sought out inspirational material, the distinctive boundaries between evangelical and non-evangelical texts were crossed. For Brown, evangelical and American popular culture intermingled, blurring cultural identities, with culture absorbing ambiguous and even contradictory ideas. Historian David Paul Nord also emphasized how the publishing activities of missionary and tract societies gave birth to an era of mass publication of popular culture. What Nord called "a finger of Providence" pointed to the coming of faith outside the canon of sacred texts.[7] In a parallel movement, visual historian David Morgan traced the evolution of pictorial materials used by Protestants during this era, noting how dispensationalists as well as Roman Catholics appropriated visual texts to promote the faith, advance piety, and evangelize others. Nineteenth-century pictures, not yet moving, combined instruction and recreation in tending religious flocks.

Other Protestant novels dotted the cultural landscape, many situated in Western locales. Harold Bell Wright, for example, was a minister-author, unabashedly evangelistic in his preaching and writing, described as "a moralist, a fabulist, a preacher of sermons, a Sayer, and an Utterer."[8] His books, called "personalized sermons," were "Taylor-made for the sentimentalized romances of moral Western film genres, with a liberal salting with specialized Nature study."[9] Sales figures marked him as one of the top best-selling novelist of the early twentieth century, and like the motion picture advertisements of Paramount Pictures, Wright's novels popped up throughout the pages of religious periodicals. Advertisement copy for *The Re-creation of Brian Kent*

7. Nord, *Faith in Reading*, 3.

8. Overton, *American Nights Entertainment*, 124.

9. Kinkead, "Western Sermons of Harold Bell Wright," 85.

boasted that "the story is as sweet and clean and wholesome as the atmosphere of the out-of-doors of God's unspoiled world," and "you must see The Shepherd of the Hills now in Ten Reel Motion Picture. Scenario and Direction in every detail by Harold Bell Wright—PERSONALLY."[10]

In 1898, Wright, a minister of the Christian Church in coal-mining Pittsburg, Kansas, had worked in close proximity to rowdy taverns and houses of prostitution. His preaching was renowned for its illustrative language and pulpit storytelling, drawing sermons from newspaper articles attacking local sins like the midway attractions that lured young girls under ten into singing vile songs. Dissatisfied with what he called "churchianity," he decided to write anecdotal narratives like *The Shepherd of the Hills* (1907) for his congregation and read them serially. His lively and popular preaching evolved into entertaining stories, even as such literary codes were being adapted to silent films. Almost twenty of Wright's novels became sensational, as well as didactic, bestsellers, thinly disguised sermons about rugged individualists, nature, noble savages, frontier women, Western experience versus education, and the inferiority of the East. His themes emphasized that true religion should be a part of daily life, not merely a Sunday ritual; that simple country folk living close to nature are morally superior to wealthy urbanites; and that the evils of the American social structure need correction by true men and true women who lived according to Christian principles.

10. *"Re-creation of Brian Kent,"* 1272.

FIGURE 4

When Presbyterian elder Will H. Hays become head of the MPPDA,
the press aptly caricatured him in the good, moral image of the
Western hero (public domain, courtesy Bruce Long, Arizona State
University).

In 1911, he wrote his most popular Western, *The Winning of Barbara Worth*, set in Imperial Valley, in a country
called La Palmos de la Mano de Dios (The Palm of the Hand
of God). A potent mix of Barbara's feminine spirituality and
the tough natural school of the desert transform an Eastern
wimp into a man of God. Like Zane Grey, Wright promoted

"standards of honor and decency and fair play"[11] as in his novel, *A Son of His Father*. The heroes are what the Western myths considered real men. The love plots waned in significance with "a good woman [being] like a good horse." The basic narrative plot of "the good boy gone bad—or turned rustler—who redeems himself before his sacrificial death . . . with exemplary death bed scenes" would also form the skeleton of many William S. Hart films.[12] His novels provided reassurance to the Protestant masses of the superiority of virtue and moral and physical strength. They were acceptable, even laudatory, guides for the morality of the young.

FIGURE 5

Producer Samuel Goldwyn financed Wright's Western melodrama promoting the moral decency of the early twentieth century (courtesy Warner Bros. Archives USC).

11. Wilkins, *Harold Bell Wright*, 1.

12. Kinkead, "Western Sermons of Harold Bell Wright," 86; for a fuller analysis of the "evangelical" Western silent films, see Lindvall, "God in the Saddle," 318.

Under the pen name of "Ralph Connor," the Reverend Charles William Gordon wrote when the West was raw, rugged, and mystical in the imaginations of Eastern authors. Blending a Canadian frontier religion with mining and lumber camps, he sketched a masculine backdrop for heroes that bore a remarkable resemblance to the emerging personality of the transformed rugged Rough Rider himself, Teddy Roosevelt.

Writing fiction was a suspect calling for a minister, so he penned missionary adventures under his *nom de plume*, drawing vivid pictures that demonstrated how evil was rooted in selfishness. In *Black Rock: A Tale of the Selkirks* (1898), saloon dancing and a traveling farce show (vaudevillian), with plenty of food and "drink" (i.e., liquor), separate miners from their money, and unfortunately, from their wives, mothers, and families. With all the gambling, Black Rock was one of those little suburbs of hell. Drunkenness and violence proliferate in this temperance tale. "Billy Breen, a drunkard reformed under the tender but firm care of the widowed Mrs. Mavor, drinks some lemonade that [the barkeeper villain] had spiked in order to regain his former customer."[13] Billy, languishing over a half-empty bottle of whiskey at this side, repents, but still dies miserably. Immorality has its vivid consequences. Yet, God haunts both the environs and people of Black Rock, as the Author of goodness and of personal transformation. The spiritual mark of the community is forgiveness, a theme that plays out consistently in the Western films of Billy Broncho and William S. Hart.

13. Ferre, *Social Gospel for Millions*, 49.

FIGURES 6–7

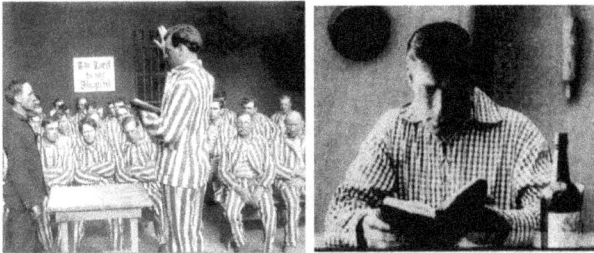

The westerns of Broncho Billy and William S. Hart brought a
Protestant sense of sin, repentance, and conversion in films like
Broncho Billy's Sentence (Gilbert M. Anderson, 1915) and *Hell's
Hinges* (1916) (courtesy Stu Minnis).

The locations in nature served as divine characters in
the Western morality plays. Like angels of death, deserts
and unpredictable storms could descend with the wrath
of God on wayward pilgrims. Preceding the mythmaking
monuments of John Ford, the wilderness of the silent film,
the West was a fitting place for God and for the smudged,
dusty image of God in the cowboy. Nature was symbolic
of the glory of God. The Hudson River School artists had
envisioned America as the new promised land. Their
"paintings—filled with light—reflect deeply held religious
convictions, expressing man's harmony with nature. Light
is the most obvious manifestation of God's presence"[14] and
light seemed more available, more ubiquitous, and more
divine in the wide-open landscapes of the West.

These western religious novels of Ralph Connor and
Harold Bell Wright, as well as their desert landscapes,
form the backdrop to Rupert Hughes's "religious" work
that sought to justify the ways of Hollywood to American

14. Cooper, *Knights of the Brush*, 3.

society. However, after the Great War, stories of sentiment and uplift gave way to more exciting and realistic narratives. It was in this context of the popularity of these religious fictions that Hughes would publish his provocative *Souls for Sale* in 1922. Instead of a red-blooded young religious man going west to assert his ministry, however, the protagonist was now a young woman yearning for freedom and meaning, turning away from her religious roots.

Late in the second decade of filmmaking, numerous films had extolled the virtues of religion, culminating in two of the top films of 1919 and 1922, George Loane Tucker's *The Miracle Man* and Lon Chaney's *Shadows*, respectively. In a letter to Arthur B. Maurice, book editor at the *New York Herald*, Hughes acknowledged the potential of great films as something akin to those works of religious fictions. Such works "have started great pilgrimages."[15] He was ready and eager to publish his parody of a spiritual journey and lead his own pilgrimage of fallen saints out to a new Holy Wood.

15. Kemm, *Literary Legacy*, 114.

2

BILLY SUNDAY
AND THE VIRTUOUS CINEMA

The earliest popular films were Passion Plays, borrowed from the mountains of Oberammergau, Austria, but filmed not only in the Holy Land, but even on the rooftops in New York City. Using startling wizardry, French stage magician turned filmmaker George Méliès astounded spectators with *Le Christ Marchant Sur les Flots* (1899) with a credibly human Jesus walking across waves toward viewers who gaped in belief. Film historian Janet Staiger surmised that pious believers might marvel at the novel apparatus that projected such images, thinking, "What a powerful sign of the Lord's beneficence and bounty to his flock!"[1] This cinema of attractions won over many clergy, Congregationalists in particular, to the illusory art of the moving picture and quickened their sense of its prophetic and educational powers.

Hollywood would later capitalize on such a tradition, with Charles Fox promulgating the image of Hollywood as

1. Staiger, "Conclusions and New Beginnings," 354.

a sacred place. "Few people know that in all this world there are but two places where an organized attempt is made to present in dramatic form the life of the Christ: Oberammergau, the tiny Bavarian village, where every ten years the inhabitants, led by Anton Lang, present the Passion Play is one of these two places. Strange as it may seem, to the person unfamiliar with Hollywood, as it really is, the other place is Hollywood itself."[2]

Leading the vanguard movement of the spiritual and educational value of the moving picture was the visionary minister of South Congregational Church in New Britain, Connecticut, the Reverend Herbert A. Jump, who in 1911 published the first significant pamphlet on moving pictures, entitled "The Religious Possibilities of the Motion Picture." Jump championed the potential of movies to tell parables, like that of Jesus' recounting of the Good Samaritan, pointing out how this dramatic story offered an example of ideal preaching, "which many preachers of the present day, alas!, seem to have completely overlooked":

> Note some of the details of that sermon-story. It was not taken from the Bible—the Old Testament used as a Bible by Jesus' auditors—but from contemporary experience. It was the sort of thing that might have happened any day and of any one in his audience. Secondly, it was an exciting story. Robber-tales always thrill the emotions, and much more in the ancient world perhaps than today, because then the risk and the likelihood of such deeds of violence were immeasurably greater than now. Thirdly, this narrative-sermon frankly introduces morally negative elements and leaves them negative to the end of the chapter. Was it not dangerous to the church establishment of that day to have its

2. Fox, *Mirrors of Hollywood*, 12.

priest and Levite pictured as failing so utterly
in the grace of compassion, held up to ridicule
as hypocrites and poseurs? And as for the rob-
bers themselves, not only did the story give a
most realistic description of precisely how they
perpetrated the cowardly crime of violence, but
it leaves them victorious in their wickedness,
scurrying off with their booty, unrepentant of
their sins, probably chuckling at the folly of the
traveler for venturing upon the notorious Jeru-
salem-Jericho road without a caravan to protect
him from the highwaymen.[3]

Jump concluded that despite these dubious character-
istics of not coming from the Hebrew Bible, being remarkably violent, and having morally negative features within it,
the visual parable of the good Samaritan portrays the heart
of the gospel more profoundly and memorably than many
sermons. The Reverend E. Boudinot Stockton's periodical
column, "The Picture in the Pulpit," in the *Moving Picture
World* would spread Jump's message to the film community,
ushering in an early golden age of church/cinema relations.[4]

Moral and religious narratives, from melodramas to
westerns, filled the movie screens of the 1910s. The photoplays of Broncho Billy and William S. Hart were almost
Presbyterian sermons, with the cowboys turning from their
sinful ways to read the Bible, repent, and fulfill a calling
to do the Lord's work. Films like *Broncho Billy's Sentence*
(Gilbert M. "Broncho Billy" Anderson, 1915) and *Hell's
Hinges* (Charles Swickard, 1916) would demonstrate how
rough men of the West could be tamed and reformed by the
gospel (often with the help of a pious, but alluring, woman
named Faith).

3. Jump, *Religious Possibilities of the Motion Picture*, 3.
4. Stockton, "Picture in the Pulpit," 336, 642–43; 983.

One popular figure who took note of the redemptive potential of the moving pictures was evangelist Billy Sunday. The enthusiastic orator decried the corrupt legitimate theater of his day, card playing, dancing, Sunday shows, and especially saloons. However, his stand on the movies was remarkably positive. Remarkably, the citizens of Norfolk, Virginia, welcomed Sunday in early 1921 for a series of revival services, in which movies offered a healthy alternative for the "city of vice" overrun with saloons and brothels.[5]

Sunday nurtured personal friendships with movie celebrities like William S. Hart, Cecil B. DeMille, and Douglas Fairbanks. Although *Variety* lamented that his popular tent revival services would be around for ten weeks, it was not because he opposed the movies as much as he drew crowds away from the movie theaters.[6] In fact, a reviewer for the *Motion Picture News*, William Lord Wright, listed several items to be grateful for as the movie industry entered the Thanksgiving season in 1912. Topping the list was "that evangelist Billy Sunday says picture shows are all right."[7] In one full-page advertisement, Sunday recommended D. W. Griffith's *Orphans of the Storm* as a "sermon of the highest value":[8] "The power of the moving picture should be used to inculcate warnings and lessons that the world needs . . . would that every story carried on the screen might have a lesson as powerful, and as useful, a motive as praiseworthy."[9]

5. Lindvall, "Sundays in Norfolk," 80.
6. "Afraid of Billy Sunday," 3.
7. Wright, *Motion Picture News*, 14.
8. "God Helps Poor Girls," 2:8.
9. "Reverend Billy Sunday Says," 10.

Billy Sunday and the Virtuous Cinema

FIGURE 8

Famed baseball star and evangelist Billy Sunday attacked saloons and sin, but approved of movies, even so much as being playfully photographed with bawdy American icon Mae West and his wife, Helen Thompson "Ma" Sunday (courtesy Culver Pictures).

An early incident with Sunday typified the mixture of the film industry's social message and the religious community's willingness to be associated with it. Director Allan Dwan was filming actor Frank Campeau as a convict searching for the man who framed him and needed a model for an Evangelist in *Jordan Is a Hard Road*, starring Dorothy Gish, Frank Campeau, and Owen Moore. He needed a technical director for the religious sequences; revivalist Billy Sunday was the man for the job as he was renowned for promulgating a vigorous brand of muscular Christianity. Dwan tells the story in his own words as follows:

> Frank Campeau had to play an Evangelist, so I
> got a fellow named Billy Sunday who was a well-
> known Evangelist, like today's Billy Graham,

and used him as my technical adviser. We put up a huge tent over in Hollywood across from the studio and filled it full of extras—not professional ones—just people off the streets. Now, in the story, Campeau is supposed to harangue them about religion and make them come to god, but I got Billy Sunday up there and he let them have one of his best hot lectures, and I had about three cameras filming only the audience. And pretty soon these people began to feel it, and the first thing you know, they were crawling up the aisles on their knees, coming up to Billy Sunday to be saved, hollering "Hallelujah" and going into hysteria. A terrific scene. No bunch of million-dollar actors could have done it. You could see the frenzy in their faces. And after we cut, he actually went on with the religious revival right there. Then I was able to put Campeau up there and let him go through the gestures of talking, cutting back all the time to these people I'd already shot. The effect was astonishing.[10]

Even more impressive was a secondary impact that Sunday's presence as a consultant for the film had on another technical advisor. Former bank robber Al Jennings advised Dwan on how to stage train and bank robberies. However, as historian Larry Langman recorded it: "Jennings became so enthralled with Sunday's message that he became a lecturer on the religious circuit, using his criminal background as the basis for his sermon." Newsreels documented the Baseball Evangelist's impact. In 1915 alone, Sunday would appear in news pictorials for Hearst-Selig, *Pathé News*, and *Animated Weekly*.[11]

10. Bogdanovich, *Allan Dwan*, 40.
11. Langman, *Guide to Silent Westerns*, 235.

Billy Sunday and the Virtuous Cinema

By the early 1920s, Billy Sunday and numerous clergy celebrated the moving picture as a handmaiden to religion. As a fundamentalist reformer, with all the vim and vigor of an athlete, Sunday denounced modernism, card playing, dancing, and alcohol. "Whiskey and beer are all right in their place," he would thunder on the sawdust trails of his tabernacle revivals, "but their place is in hell."[12] In contrast to the saloons, brothels, and the legitimate theater, the movie theater for Sunday was downright wholesome and virtuous. Its reputation would turn, however, with a few Hollywood scandals.

FIGURE 9

The World's Renowned Evangelist

THE REV. **BILLY SUNDAY**

See Him in Motion Pictures

ONE SOLID REEL
LIFE THROBBING ACTIONS
Each gesture appropriate to his striking sayings

The Billy Sundaygrams have reformed thousands
The livest Reel you have shown on your screen.

Block One and Three Sheets
WRITE OR WIRE FOR TERRITORY
IT'S GOING FAST!

LEWIS-WOLFF CO., 110 West 40 St., New York

Billy Sunday not only recommended certain films, but was frequently documented in newsreels and "Sundaygrams" ("Advertisement for Billy Sunday Films" *Motion Picture News* 11 (915) 69; courtesy Library of Congress).

Until after the World War, Victorian sensibilities ruled Hollywood. However, cracks appeared in the respectable

12. Ellis, *Billy Sunday*, 66.

Protestant culture. In their classic sociological study of Muncie, Indiana, *Middleton* (1939), Robert and Helen Lynd chronicled the changes of lifestyle from the 1890s through the 1920s on the modest Midwestern town. Historian Lary May cited one particular trend: "On Sunday, previously characterized by strict Protestant mores and the absence of amusements, the movies gathered their largest audiences, outnumbering the city's churchgoers."[13] Movies were to mark "progressive" cultural changes (e.g., temperance movements, child labor laws, women suffrage, and urban reform) and to abet them as agents of change themselves.

Christian groups, from the Salvation Army to the *Christian Herald* magazine, were engaged in producing movies for churches.[14] The Methodist Episcopal Church held its largest outdoor centennial celebration in 1919 in Columbus, Ohio, at which they exhibited, on a giant 136-foot by 146-foot screen, thousands of films as a means to educate and evangelize. Sheldon's notable essay on "In His Steps Today: What Would Jesus Do with the Drama," explored in detail what Jesus's responses would be. The Savior enters as a character among a dramatist, a manager, an actor, and the public to demonstrate how God redeems everything for his purposes. Church leaders summoned fellow clergy to use movies for missions and for the church to become a social recreational center in the community. Even *The Literary Digest* envisioned films as religion's handmaiden, suggesting that pictures in the pulpit would increase attendance ("pictures in the pulpit mean more people in the pews)" and that the church could "wrest another weapon from the devil and convert it to its own purpose."[15] What all of this augured was an optimistic view of the moving

13. May, *Screening Out the Past*, xi.

14. Lindvall, *Sanctuary Cinema*, 117.

15. "Motion Picture as a Handmaiden of Religion," 46–47.

pictures as a virtuous medium intended for God's glory and the social rest of his people. However, the moving pictures would prove to be a very fallible instrument of the Lord.

3

A MODERNIST TURN AND
HOLLYWOOD SCANDALS

A t the turn of the century, the church carried scars from slashing wits, satirists, and bitter critics for its hypocrisy and cant. Militant atheist Robert G. Ingersoll fumed at the intolerant lunatics of Christianity. Mark Twain turned from his folksy riverboat humor toward a more scathing critique of religious people in works like his "War Prayer," where he blasted the jingoistic conspiracy of politics and religion. He would lambaste his Presbyterian upbringing by describing man as the only religious animal with the True Religion, several of them. Ambrose Bierce scribbled his clever cynicism through *The Devil's Dictionary* published in 1911, believing that the true function of wit was not to "make one writhe with merriment, but with anguish" and shot his venomous quills at specific individuals and not mere abstractions. Preachers were merely "birds of prey." He redefined a clergyman as "one who undertakes their management of our spiritual affairs as a method of bettering his temporal ones."[1] His poem entitled "Christian" introduces

1. Bierce, *Devil's Dictionary*, 14.

a man who is not a "Christian," as he is Christ himself. For Bierce, the idea of attacking the sin, but sparing the sinner was stupid and ineffective. He would retort, "Why spare the sinner?"[2] He essentially opined that it would take all the fun, however venomous, from the task of reformation.

Journalist H. L. Mencken would become the "public immoralist" of the 1920s, "the heaver of dead cats into the sanctuaries of America" and a man who "when he smelled flowers, looked for a coffin."[3] Perhaps he alone chewed up the fundamentalists so much at the Scopes Trial in 1925 that they retreated from culture and would not peek their heads out until they grew into evangelicals in the 1970s. Such satiric attacks on the church would inform Hughes's tweaking of the religious nose in his scathing writings against God's chosen people.

The church itself was in the throes of a major division between fundamentalists and modernists at the turn of the decade. The controversy arose most visibly in the Presbyterian Church in the United States of America, where doctrines about the inspiration of the Scriptures (and inerrancy), the historical reality of Christ's miracles, the virgin birth, the death of Christ as an atonement for sin, and the bodily resurrection of Jesus were disputed. These five fundamental propositions would underlie the emergence of fundamentalists at Princeton Seminary. Other progressive Presbyterians who helped found the Federal Council of Churches, like Robert E. Speer and Union Theological Seminary professor William Adams Brown, sought to build a church union with other denominations through an Interchurch World Movement (IWM), but were thwarted by Princeton Theological Seminary's Old School Faculty, led by J. Gresham Machen.

2. Bierce, *Collected Works*, 10:98.

3. Lindvall, *God Mocks*, 213.

Historian William H. Romanowski astutely points out how denominational markers are not particularly helpful when it comes to assessing a religious person's relation to the movies. The zealous Wilbur Craft (who attacked movies as "schools of vice and crime that offered children five-cent trips to hell"), Orrin G. Cocks of the National Board of Review and Will Hays, president of the Motion Picture Producers and Distributors Associations, were Presbyterian. What would be distinguishing would be their theological and cultural "*perspectives.*"[4]

FIGURE 10

OHIO STATE JOURNAL   Feb. 5, 1922

The movie industry desperately drafted Presbyterian elder
Will Hays to oversee the moral content of Hollywood films,
even as it slipped into several scandals
(public domain; courtesy Bruce Long).

4. For Romanowski, the key dynamic was a tension between "the film industry's interest in profit margins and the church's concern to protect civil liberties and the public welfare" (*Reforming Hollywood*, 8).

A Modernist Turn and Hollywood Scandals

A decisive schism occurred that highlighted these perspectives when ordained Baptist minister, the eloquent Harry Emerson Fosdick preached "Shall the Fundamentalists Win?" on May 21, 1922, marking a distinct caricature of both sides, enlightened, but unbelieving, modernists versus intolerant fundamentalists. Church historian Martin Marty identified what he saw as the main drama of the era being the climactic struggle over the role of the once imperial Protestantism.[5] Liberal Protestantism exulted in an era of confidence, as liberal Methodist bishops averred in May 1920 that "tomorrow will be every way better." The dream of Protestant unity sought to move beyond tradition and "stifling" ancient creeds. Curiously, Unitarians found Roman Catholics and fundamentalists to be clergy of integrity; the progressive Protestants were "compromising and cheap," adapting to progressive zeitgeists, whatever they might be. Like fundamentalists, Roman Catholics remained adamantly anti-modernist. Even naturalists like University of Chicago philosopher Henry Nelson Wieman looked askance at liberals, challenging the view of a modernist Christianity by saying "that this is not a nice world and God is not a nice God."[6] Moderns adopted a Versailles mentality, where we have ended the war to end all wars and the time is ripe for a League of Religions as well as Nations. However, World War I should have stomped all optimism out of liberalism, but it would take another, more horrific, war to do that.

Modernists from the Federal Council of the Churches publicized how motion pictures could be effectively employed in religion and educational work. With its "wholehearted approval," it "sanctioned" the photoplay as an uplifting form of public entertainment, based on the idea

5. Marty, *Modern American Religion*, 2.
6. Marty, *Modern American Religion*, 198, 200.

that "human nature is good and when it has the opportunity to choose between the higher and lower, all other things being equal, it will choose the former."[7] Other liberals championed the idea that "If Christ Went to the Movies," he would approve, being overjoyed because "Christ approves of anything that makes for the happiness of mankind." The article showcased New York author Cleveland Moffett, who promoted an "ideal church" with free moving picture entertainment. Such "broad-minded" churchmen enabled Christ to say about the movies: "Let my people enjoy this thing. . . . Blessed be that which uplifts, restores, and refreshes the weary souls of men."[8] Modern churchmen were preoccupied with social welfare, paramount being the mental and social health of the poor, which movies could now provide. Such statements fit what Charles Clayton Morrison, editor of the *Christian Century* (which believed the 1900s would be such a triumphant Protestant era that they changed their periodical title to it) saw two worlds clashing: "the world of tradition and the world of modernism. One is scholastic, static, authoritarian, individualistic; the other is vital, dynamic, free, social."[9] And one key to this new age was the dynamism of the machine, of science (even forms of social Darwinism and evolution) and modern technology, of which moving pictures were primary evidence of progress. Conservative Presbyterian professor at Princeton Theological Seminary, J. Gresham Machen, concluded in his *Christianity and Liberalism* (1923) that "liberal theology was, in fact, a new religion."[10]

7. McConoughey, "Motion Pictures in Religious and Educational Work," 3–4.

8. Grant, "If Christ Went to the Movies," 29–30.

9. Marty, *Modern American Religion*, 201.

10. Butler, *Religion in American Life*, 349.

Modernity embraced the imports of German idealism and biblical higher criticism, articulating what they saw a "mediating theology." A liberal Protestant mass culture assumed hegemony in the postwar evolution of American culture, dictating individual and social morality over theology. Connected as well with the Chautauqua Movement, it celebrated a quote from reformer Washington Gladden in that "amusement, like religion and education, is a real need of human beings."[11]

FIGURE 11

The devil not only leads the Destructive Critics of Academia, but also Unitarians, Christian Scientists, Spiritualists, and the Movie Crowd (caricatured as Charlie Chaplin and Ben Turpin) to hell (Grover Martin, "On the Way," *King's Business* 12 [1921] 1184; courtesy Biola University).

Fundamentalists began to divorce themselves from this new idolatry, and began to clamor for federal censorship. Some, like conservative Baptist T. C. Horton, attacked the same modernist Reverend Cleveland Moffett for

11. Rieser, *Chautauqua Moment*, 362.

embracing the new medium as a path to the "house of the harlot" and a "gate to hell."[12] Hollywood identified fundamentalists as easier prey for a liberal Hollywood culture, especially as the two theological groups began to differ on the direction that the movies were taking. What remained unnoticed was how much mammon mixed with modernity. As industrial production soared, with surplus capital pouring into the stock market, money tempted everyone.

FIGURE 12

CLEVELAND MOFFETT'S IDEAL CHURCH

Fundamentalists attacked the Modernist church of the Reverend Moffett as much for their church movies as their "New Theology" (T. C. Horton, "Cleveland Moffett's Ideal Church," *King's Business* 10 [1919] 395; courtesy Biola University).

12. Horton, "Cleveland Moffett's Crazy Quilt," 395–96.

A Modernist Turn and Hollywood Scandals

Hollywood was not safe from its own critics. Director Cecil B. DeMille, who would later produce such biblical blockbusters as *The Ten Commandments* (Paramount, 1923) and *King of Kings* (Pathe Exchange, 1927), was busy titillating spectators by the late teens. His scandalously suggestive titles like *Old Wives for New* (Paramount, 1918) and *Don't Change Your Husband* (Paramount, 1919) followed a postwar relaxation of Victorian sensibilities. Even though cautionary moral tales, they teased audiences with luxurious bathrooms and new moralities. However, such vicarious temptations portraying excessive drinking, partying, divorce, and consumption, a stage was set for an actual scandal. On September 3, 1921, Hollywood fell into sin and came under direct assault. The California DA indicted the delightfully popular comedian Roscoe "Fatty" Arbuckle for the alleged rape and murder of starlet Virginia Rappe at wild party in San Francisco. Even though later exonerated on all charges, the Hearst press pilloried Arbuckle and all of Hollywood, which would suffer several other indignities.

The wholesome actor Wallace Reid overdosed on morphine and died in a sanitarium, while director William Desmond Taylor (who had directed Hughes's 1918 scenario of *Johanna Enlists*) was mysteriously murdered. Subsequent investigations implicated other actresses, such as spunky actress Mabel Normand (whose cocaine addiction had seemingly been abetted by Taylor). Such scandals unleashed numerous editorial cartoons and sermons on the evils of the film industry. One particularly sensational and anti-Semitic book, entitled *The Sins of Hollywood* (1922), introduced "a Group of Stories of Actual Happenings Reported and Written by a Hollywood Newspaper Man." It covered everything from strip poker and paddle parties to sodomy and murder, culminating in a leering Jewish filmmaker hounding a vulnerable starlet.

FIGURE 13

The cover of a 1922 exposé imagined the worst of the intersection of Hollywood and vice (public domain).

Industry leaders battled attacks on at least two major fronts. First, critics denounced movies as a mere industry rather than an art. Second, due to the Arbuckle scandal, reformers mounted a campaign against movies, including disputes over censorship and Sunday blue law showings. The Presbyterian Church sought to unite moral agencies in May 1922 to bring about federal legislation to regulate film content. Hollywood responded by circling the wagons to respond to this religious intrusion and by showing how movies provided uplift to the nation. A columnist reported that Hollywood celebrities invited Hughes to join them in their fight against these East coast blue bloods.[13]

With poet/critic Vachel Lindsay and others, Hughes defended moving pictures as a new art, as drama once was. For Hughes, such "art required a kind of celibacy as some religions did."[14] He confessed that "most films are inartistic in their result, though most of them are artistic in their purpose and effort [like many novels]. What annoys me in the criticism of the movies is the superior attitude assumed by its scorners." He believed that the motion picture camera had become so highly developed that it is as agile and as flexible as a chisel, a brush, a violin bow, or a fountain pen. "If critics would treat pictures as they do other works of art, expecting a general dead level, a common mediocrity, and eagerly seeking and praising the high moments, we and they would all be a lot happier." When a famous painter arrived on his set for *Remembrance*, Hughes noted that the famous artist cried out, "That is the most poignant face I ever saw. That face converts me to the movies."[15]

When praising the art form of the moving pictures, Hughes highlighted certain great movies such as *The Cabinet of Dr. Caligari* (1920), which seemed to spring "full armed from the brow of Jove, just as the drama did." So, too, was Griffith's racist *Birth of a Nation* a gigantic classic for Hughes, along with those passionate hunters of beauty and emotion, the DeMilles. Hughes was not shy in directing the

13. "Movie Men Favor a Federal Censor," 2:1. Beside the issue of censorship, Hughes tackles what he saw as the more pressing concern of blue laws and Sunday showings. In the Midwest town of Calverly, the campaign "to close the motion picture houses on Sunday was lost at the last election. The church is closed."

14. Hughes, *Souls for Sale*, 378.

15. "Movie-Making an Art," 8:3.

glory towards the writers when one of his fictional filmmakers spouts: "We are like the Greeks, like the men of Chaucer's time, and Shakespeare's time and Fielding's. We're presiding at the birth of an immortal art. Some of us don't know it. But posterity will know it. We're among the immortals!" The true "cinemite" would go forth on a crusade like "Peter the Eremite to summon people to her banner of rescue, of sympathy, of ardor." One needed to reclaim the holy land of moving pictures, to lift high the flag of Goldwyn's "*ars gratis ars*." One senses that Hughes's summons carried a touch of irony in calling for a "crusade." He would now be working with the producer whose aphorisms, however apocryphal, are legendary, such as "We want a story that starts out with an earthquake and works its way up to a climax," and "It's more than magnificent—it's mediocre."[16]

In an article entitled "The Art of Moving Picture Composition," Hughes berated the scorn of the "sophomorons" and "moviephobes" who disparaged film, who thought that by "elevating their eyebrows and nose they elevate their point of view."[17] Again, he pointed to the recent aesthetic virtues of expressionistic German films as evidence for the art's development. Delineating how he himself composed with the camera, Hughes drew upon his directorial skills as a landscape painter, immodestly praising his own compositional arrangements of desert scenes and one particular image of Mem standing before a cross out in the desolate brush of the southwest.[18]

Hughes equated the aesthetic design of his earlier films with such artists as Degas, Teniers, and Whistler. Now, he boasted that since his *Souls for Sale* was about filmmaking, it would allow him to pose his actress before a bank

16. Hughes, *Souls for Sale*, 269, 285.
17. Hughes, "Art of Moving Picture Composition," 9–10.
18. Hughes, "Art of Moving Picture Composition," 92.

of Cooper-Hewitt tubes or a blinding Winfield to evoke a "Rembrandtesque frame of black around a core of such dazzling radiance that the girl's features were lost in shimmering radiance."[19] Hughes showed no lack of confidence in his own abilities to further this novel art.

In another essay, entitled "The Necessity for Originality in Photo-Plays," Hughes articulated that the greatest appeal of the photoplay in this its pioneer stage was its ability to reveal "casual bits of graphic human veracity, a touch of character, or of sympathy, or of vivid realty." What this would lead to, however, was an exposé of the frailty of all humanity. The censors would seem to pretend that there was never any wickedness in the world until pictures began to move, but, Hughes reiterated, the camera functioned as a "marvelous instrument of expression" for disclosing humanity to humanity.[20] While it could illustrate simple homely pathos or humor, it could also bare the heart of all humanity.

In comic contrast, the successful Hollywood screenwriter Anita Loos and her minister husband, John Emerson, scribbled their own version of the sources of inspiration for writing photoplay scenarios: "plot-germs are everywhere."[21] Most authors held higher estimates of their calling among the vulgar film folk. Samuel Goldwyn went out to hire "Eminent Authors," what he simply called "classy writers"; yet out of the legion of aspiring scriptwriters, only two "beat the game: Rex Beach and Rupert Hughes delivered both the prestige and the audiences Goldwyn sought."[22]

The early 1920s was a heyday of aggressive public relations for Hollywood. In the 1924 publication, *The Truth*

---

19. Hughes, "Art of Moving Picture Composition," 92.
20. Hughes, "Necessity for Originality in Photo-Plays," 375.
21. Emerson and Loos, *How to Write Photo-Plays*, 7.
22. Berg, *Goldwyn*, 92.

about the Movies by the Stars, Laurence Hughes (no relation) propped up Hollywood as the "City of Churches" with over fifty denominations represented. It was a conservative, Anglo-Saxon center of religious communities, and only a few minor scandals had tainted its image. Trying to purify the public perception of Hollywood, the pamphlet's loving and respectful dedication applauds "all those who labor with soul and mind and body that the rest of us may find spiritual and emotional entertainment in the films" and also those who supply "the TRUTH," impartial and unbiased, for readers for whom "there is a way. The Truth is the way and, in this book, the torch of Truth has been held before you" so that you may see if you have it in you to be a star.[23] The language is unapologetically and blatantly biblical, almost a parody of Jesus' words that he is the "way, the truth, and the life."

The essay "What about the Morals of Hollywood?" directly asked: Is Hollywood "wicked" and a "seething maelstrom of unmentionable Vice?"[24] The answer is unabashedly evangelistic: "Do you think that, in Hollywood, there are no Churches where Christ and his gospel are preached? Do you understand the meaning of that great philosopher and teacher who trod the pathways of Palestine many years ago, when he said 'He that is without sin among you, let him first cast a stone.'" The essay appeals to the morality of Jesus Christ against those who have "elected, falsely, maliciously, venomously, to slander and agonize and take away the reputations of men and women of decency and morality, —true morality—broad minded and cosmopolitan morality—the morality that loves and tolerates and understands human weakness."[25] Hollywood seemingly had a friend in Jesus.

23. Hughes, *Truth about the Movies*, 5, 11, 17.
24. De Courssey, "What about the Morals of Hollywood," 31.
25. De Courssey, "What about the Morals of Hollywood," 32–33.

A Modernist Turn and Hollywood Scandals

In another direct salvo in 1923, Hollywood business-men Laurance Hill and Silas Snyder, writing for the *Los Angeles Times*, published their *Can Anything Good Come Out of Hollywood?* It brazenly played off an undisguised allusion to its biblical source, namely the disciple Nathaniel's question regarding Jesus, "Can anything good come out of Nazareth?" and its apt response, "Come and *see*."[26] The authors mounted a campaign to show the centrality of the Christian religion in the Hollywood community, where Wesley's hymn, "Christ the Lord Is Risen Today" is sung in the Hollywood bowl and Christmas is celebrated as in every other American community. In an undisguised allusion to the gospel story, they invited their readers: "*Come and see* Hollywood." It was a shameless commercial exploiting Scripture itself.

Like these propagandists, Hughes set up his well-devised dialectic between the church and Hollywood, eventually culminating in a convenient marriage of heaven and hell. What he articulated in numerous essays would be translated into his histrionic narrative.

26. Hill and Snyder, *Can Anything Good Come Out of Hollywood?*, 58.

4

THE BIRTH OF A NOVEL

Rupert Hughes's novel was an unabashed defense of Hollywood people against H. L. Mencken's Midwestern religious "boob-oisie."[1] Annoyed at what he saw as a double standard, he attacked the spurious moral superiority of religious persons and inadvertently reaffirmed the democratic doctrine of the sinful nature of all human beings. He framed the question in his novel as "Are the moving picture people very wicked?"[2]

To counter the accusations against the Hollywood scandals, Hughes cited literary evidence and press clippings of the disastrous affairs of churchmen and their communicants, stemming back to the days of the infamous Henry Ward Beecher affair. He drew up a list of religious crimes, of Protestants beating Roman Catholics to death, of a violent faith healer, of ministers drowning wives and flogging children; "yet nobody dreamed of assailing religion as an incentive to murder; no one warned the young to avoid churches or suggested a censorship of sermons." Echoes of

1. Lopez, "Writing Mencken."
2. Hughes, *Souls for Sale*, 143.

Ingersoll's cynical inquiry "Why should I allow that same god to tell me how to raise my kids, who had to drown his own?" rippled throughout his rhetoric.

Hughes fervently denounced those who throw the first stone:

> An actor involved in a dull revel, of a sort infinitely frequent since mankind first encountered alcohol, was present at the death of an actress. The first versions of the disaster were so horribly garbled that the nation was shaken with horror. All the simmering resentment against the evil elements and ugly excesses of the "fifth largest industry in the world" boiled over in a scalding denunciation of the entire motion picture populace. For a week or two the nation rose in one mob to lynch an entire craft and all its folk. Editors, politicians, reformers, preachers, clubwomen, all of those who make a career of denunciation and take a pride in what they detest, drew up a blanket indictment against thousands of assorted souls and condemned them to infamy. There was a deacon in our church, a good man as ever was, but now and then he'd go mad for liquor, and he never knew what he might do. Once, after a long period of being perfectly nice, he tasted the communion wine and left the church and went mad crazy with whiskey.[3]

The Arbuckle scandal was a *cause celebre* monopolizing the headlines during the time of Hughes's writing, tarring and feathering Hollywood with fantasies of being a Bacchic revel or decadent debauch. Sex was at the forefront of every newspaper article.[4] Interweaving the facts of the vast popularity and subsequent outrage of this

3. Hughes, *Souls for Sale*, 247.
4. Lindvall, "The Organ in the Sanctuary," 139.

"comedian of Falstaffian girth" amid the fiction of his narrative, Hughes levels vehement criticisms against the ambitious district attorney (a "pitiful, hateful, lamentable attack") and then segues into a concurrent cry against censorship.

The contrast would be embodied by his heroine Mem's rescue in the desert by the larger-than-life western actor, Tom Holby. His help makes her feel like "the Magdalen in the pictures, though the man who looked down upon her so tenderly had never posed as a Galilean, even in the Miracle Play they give every summer in the canyon of Hollywood." Hughes makes sure that two points are not lost: first, he situates the Passion Play in his sacred land Hollywood and second, he explicitly contrasts Holby's profession as an actor to a preacher's admonitory task: in his movies, Holby "tried to show how people actually did behave, not how they ought to."

The author's libertarian key to it all is to live and let live. Hughes appeals to the actor's vocation of making others happy as the fundamental ethical principle of all life. As has been mentioned, in March 1920, the Reverend Dr. Percy Stickney Grant, a self-described "broad-minded clergyman," defender of socialism and liberal divorce laws, caught the liberal spirit of the day in an article in *Photoplay* magazine entitled "If Christ Went to the Movies." Grant's therapeutic theology coincided with Hughes's religion devoid of any supernatural aspects as Grant concluded that if Christ did go to the movies, "He would approve," because the One who sought to take away the burdens of others basically wanted people to be happy, and the movies made people happy. "Christ approves of anything that makes for the happiness of mankind."[5] Remember tries to figure out why conservatives viewed moving pictures as abhorrent. Movie people were "merely trying to illuminate life, to pass

5. Grant, "If Christ Went to the Movies," 29–30, 121.

dull hours away, to quicken the spirits of the lonely and the weary." They were, in her opinion, basically, like this man from Galilee who wanted everyone to have a good time.

FIGURE 14

The Reverend Dr. Percy Stickney Grant celebrated a broad religious faith that made people happy, as Christ would approve of anything that "uplifts, restores, and refreshes the weary souls of men" ("The Broad Churchman," *Photoplay* 17 [1920] 29; courtesy Library of Congress).

In the new century, religion had been demythologized by the higher biblical criticism of German theologians like Rudolph Bultmann. Now movies housed the miraculous, demonstrating them with aplomb. As poet Vachel Lindsay praised the religious spectacular photoplays, he entreated the "most skeptical reader of [his] book to assume that miracles in a Biblical sense have occurred," as nature was its witness. The multitude of the miraculous was astounding: movies make men sober; they make girls prettier; they can show Jesus walking on water; and they can make a mute girl speak. For materialist Hughes, science had directly answered the prayer of poet Robert Burns, "oh, wad some power the giftie gie us to see oursel's as ithers see us," by giving us the technology of movies. Now Hughes believed we could truly see human nature through this art of mimicry.[6]

Authors, in particular, assumed the mantle as "miracle workers of a peculiar mystery, creators who spun out little universes at their own sweet will." Hughes listed his gospel movie writers, Jeanie McPherson, John Emerson, Anita Loos, June Mathis, and other scenario photo-playwrights, who had come to Los Angeles to trade "their messes of pottage for their birthrights of wealth and renown." Of course, likening these to a guild of Esau was not a biblical compliment. The chief officer of the new Writers' Club and a leading spirit of the Screen Writers' Guild (roles inaugurated by Hughes in real life), Miss Driscoll, celebrates the "Pagan Polytheism of Hollywood, with goat-legged, shaggy Pan and Jupiter carrying off Europa at dances." Driscoll wants to write scenarios for Mem. As Hughes viewed scenario writers (even himself) as the "pioneers, the Argonauts, the discoverers," he boasted of the "wiles of story makers" for whom lying was a "work of art." The pantheon on which such writers would stand was paramount.[7]

Hollywood had its own filmmaking missionaries, like Lois Weber. Her cinematic indictment of *Hypocrites* (1915) castigated wealthy and indulgence churchgoers. Hughes set up his narrative to mock those same bogus saints.

6. Lindsay, *Art of the Moving Picture* 6, 251, 305; Lindvall, *Sanctuary Cinema*, 211–12.

7. Hughes, *Souls for Sale*, 354, 71, 105.

The Spanish missionaries may have called it the City of Angels; but the moving pictures have changed its name to *Los Diablos*! For it is the central factory of Satan and his minions, the enemy of our homes, the corrupter of our young men and women—the school of crime.[8]

FIGURE 15

WHAT THE "ANGEL" MOTHER SHOULD DO TO HER "ANGELIC" CHILD!

DENVER POST   Feb. 10, 1922

Hollywood had become the naughty and debauched child of the City of Angels (public domain, courtesy Bruce Long, Arizona State University).

Hughes throws down a gauntlet to challenge the Protestant culture of the 1920s as he opens his provocative novel, *Souls for Sale*. The man who would be honored at a tribute given in his honor in 1950 by the *Los Angeles Times* (and a host of celebrities—Pat O'Brien, Governor Earl

8. Hughes, *Souls for Sale*, back cover.

Warren, and Louis B. Mayer), toasted as an exemplary "author, historian, musician, soldier," Hughes was a champion of his diabolical city of Hollywood. Not only had he written over fifty scripts adapted to screen, but he also boasted of being a neophyte Hollywood director and the notable uncle of the notorious recluse, Howard Hughes.[9]

Hughes's novel reads like an early cliff-hanging serial with plot twists and turns at the end of every chapter and sermonic bromides tossed in for moral uplift. His work masquerades as moral discourse, arguing for the virtues of the *City of Angels* against the religious establishment's damnation of *Los Diablos*, the home of the devil itself. Yet, his novel and its adaptation into a film he would himself direct, both notable failures, were nuanced assessments of a changing culture in the 1920s, and became the template for future accusations against Hollywood *and* against fundamentalism. As such, the satiric *Souls for Sale* ironically sold a bill of stereotypes that persisted for decades.

FIGURE 16

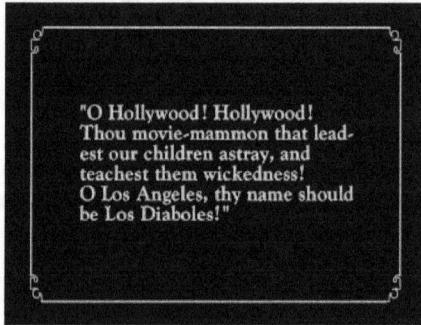

"O Hollywood! Hollywood!
Thou movie-mammon that leadest our children astray, and teachest them wickedness!
O Los Angeles, thy name should be Los Diaboles!"

**Hughes's intertitle slyly exaggerates the public perceptions of Hollywood, the city of fallen angels
(courtesy Stu Minnis).**

9. "Hughes," 1:2.

The Birth of a Novel

Hughes began writing for the movies in 1907. In 1912, his friend, Thomas Edison, approached him about adapting a story published in the *Saturday Evening Post* for his first talking picture. Hughes began making significant sums of money for his published and unpublished stories, culminating in a $50,000 profit in 1921 for the sale of his *The Old Nest*. The 1922, *Photoplay Plot Encyclopedia* praised Hughes's masterly hand in writing the story and continuity for *Dangerous Curves Ahead*, with its narrative structure typifying a new "highly specialized departure in the annals of screen-craft" and constituting a fresh plotline model that could become "average and fairly representative" for budding writers.[10] Such writings would be a mere preface for his foray into *Souls for Sale*.

FIGURES 17–18

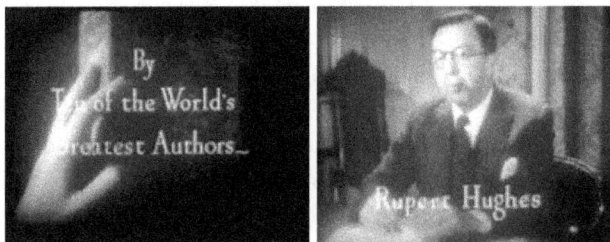

Even the Goldwyn newsreels puffed the reputation of author Rupert Hughes, garnering praise for his writing novels and film scenarios (public domain).

Receiving an MA in music and literature from Yale University, Rupert Hughes found his special calling in writing. As a chief assistant editor of the *Historians' History of the World* (in 25 volumes), he had delved into modern higher critical research. Writing became his religion.

10. Palmer, *Photoplay Plot Encyclopedia*, 53–54.

His typical Midwestern upbringing shaped his attitudes and his writings. Attending a Congregational church and numerous Sunday school picnics, saying his prayers, and diligently reading the Scriptures marked the formation of both his ideas and a distinctive moral style as well. A "fiery evangelist of Methodist persuasion" kindled his faith at an anxious bench, the front church pew where sinners saw the light.[11] The heroine's father's pulpit is referred to as his own fiery chariot. Hughes's knowledge of the Bible is quite evident in the text of his novel, showing a familiarity with minor characters like the lying Sapphira and even an apocryphal, extrabiblical, legend like Lilith, who mocks his gray Puritan heroine.[12]

However, it was at Yale where he acknowledged, "My college studies taught me that the Bible was absolutely unbelievable as a book of fact." He confessed that devolving as an ardent student of the Bible, he now was in a "state of collapse as a Christian," becoming a skeptic who would question everything and take up smoking.[13] Along with Voltaire, he believed he saw no correlation between one's beliefs and one's character, finding new heroes in "infidels" like Thomas Jefferson. According to his biographer (and admiring and devoted distant cousin) James O. Kemm, what impressed Hughes deeply as he researched the *Historians' History of the World*, as it had Robert Ingersoll before him, was the perennial atheist argument that "the worst crimes in every

11. Hughes, "Why I Quit," 7.

12. Hughes found reading the Song of Solomon's "lusciously lascivious amorous anatomy," which he found too voluptuous and erotic for a boy so young, and found such reading "appallingly hypocritical." However, not all of Hughes's biblical knowledge was lucid. In one of the stranger passages, Hughes's heroine feels "a desire to nourish her father even as Lot's daughters had nourished their father," which in the biblical text of Genesis meant incest. Or maybe he was aware.

13. Kemm, *Rupert Hughes*, 18.

nation were committed in the name of religion by religious people."[14] This would become a primary theme in his fiction, as he sought to emphasize that religion was a refuge of scoundrels, bigots, and idiots, an accusation that travels back to the second-century Greek opponent of Christianity, Celsus. His attitude parroted Ingersoll's sarcasm in that "Many people think they have religion when they are troubled with dyspepsia."[15] Religion became his *bete noir* and the clergy a suspect vocation. Hughes once explained his research methods to *New York Herald* book editor, Arthur Maurice: "As to the manners and morals of the time, I found the biographies of ministers particularly fruitful. The parsons always berate their own times and are granted a freedom of expression and an unrestrained license of denunciation not permitted to men of other trades."[16]

In an essay entitled "Why I Quit Going to Church," the iconoclast Hughes laid out his indictment of churches, preachers, and God himself. Like the mystic universalist Emanuel Swedenborg, he rejected the concept of a judgment that would damn people. He could not stomach a God who could devise and conduct such an infamous institution as hell. He found Christ's parables "ghastly" in the selective salvation of only some Jews. Religious periodicals, such as Methodist's *The Churchman* and *Current Opinion*, reacted to the "vehemence of his recent onslaught on Christianity." He responded with an article entitled "Am I an Atheist?" for which the answer was a meek acknowledgment that he was

14. Hughes, "Why I Quit," 20; "One of my greatest reasons for giving up going to church is my belief that the pulpit is the greatest power ever known for persecution, bigotry, ignorance, dishonesty, and reaction."

15. Ingersoll, *Liberty of Man, Woman and Child* (1877), "It may be that ministers really think that their prayers do good and it may be that frogs imagine that their croaking brings spring."

16. Kemm, *Rupert Hughes*, 138.

a "heathen."[17] Near the end of his life, he confessed, "I am a 'humanist' as opposed to 'divinist,' may I say? I am an atheist. I am certainly not theistic," although he continually and sincerely wished that God would bless his friends.[18] Having such an anti-religious statement published during the same time as the production of *Souls for Sale* provides a boon of insight, as the atheist apologetic and the fictional narrative parallel each other.

FIGURE 19

FREETHOUGHT OF THE DAY

"As for those who protest that I am robbing people of the great comfort and consolation they gain from Christianity, I can only say that Christianity includes hell, eternal torture for the vast majority of humanity, for most of your relatives and friends."

Rupert Hughes

"Why I Quit Going to Church" (1924)

FFRF.ORG FREEDOM FROM RELIGION FOUNDATION

Advertisement of Hughes speaking on "Why I Quit Going to Church" from the Freedom From Religion Foundation (1924) (public domain).

While mobilizing opinion on the war for the Creel Commission, he recognized the limits of censorship and

17. Hughes "Why I Quit," 144; Kemm, *Rupert Hughes*, 43, 156, 196.

18. Hughes, "Are You a Humanist?"

championed voluntary controls. He believed that censorship laws were wrongheaded attempts to "save souls by preventing them from reading, seeing, or hearing. It can't be done."[19] In 1921, he would write a satirical short subject on censorship for Douglas Fairbanks entitled "Non-Sense of Censorship," in which actor Rupert Brooke complains that, "the Motion picture is about fifteen years old. Sin is somewhat older than that, yet the censors would have us believe that it was not Satan, but Thomas A. Edison who invented 'the fall of man.'"[20] In a previous issue of *Variety*, an editorial blasted "fanatics—religious and otherwise—professional reformers and certain members of the clergy who believe they have been divinely ordained to make the United States of America holier than the holy land itself."[21] Hughes's sentiments did not thrive in a vacuum.

The 1916 serial, *Gloria's Romance*, provided an opportunity to write scenarios explicitly for the photoplay. Hollywood had adapted his other novels. Then, in 1919, the scarcely literate producer Samuel Goldfish/Goldwyn made an unprecedented move. With writer Rex Beach (*The Spoilers*), he organized a division of famous "classy" writers called the Eminent Authors, who would supervise the adaptation of their own stories.[22] Rupert Hughes was undoubtedly their star, although he admitted that he could not recognize "one entire incident, theme, or characterization" in previous adaptation of his own stories. He would direct seven films for Goldwyn, with "his name displayed prominently in advertising and title cards, as in 'Goldwyn presents a Rupert Hughes picture *Look Your Best* with

19. Kemm, *Rupert Hughes*, 103.

20. "Fairbanks Heads 'Non-Sense' Film," 44.

21. "Words from Wise in Washington," 47.

22. "Eminent Authors Pictures Formed," 1469; Berg, *Goldwyn*, 92.

Colleen Moore and Antonio Moreno. Written and Directed by Rupert Hughes."[23] Coming attraction previews would soon herald, "Coming soon, Goldwyn's stupendous production of Rupert Hughes' sensational novel, *Souls for Sale*, the story of a Movie Star in Hollywood."[24]

Goldwyn, who regarded the writer as the "most significant single contributor to a film's artistic success," attracted Hughes, whom historian Kevin Brownlow noted was the "most valuable" of the lot.[25] Goldwyn sent them all to Hollywood to "study film techniques," although the enterprise would be abandoned after a notable lack of success. The producer realized it was more difficult to convert talented writers into competent filmmakers than turning alchemist dross into gold.[26] The *New York Times* noted that among the writers who have gone into the movies, "Rupert Hughes is conspicuous by his work—where words have been his main medium, his pictures speak."[27]

Being lured to Hollywood by Goldwyn (Hughes confessed to falling under the "combined hypnosis" of Goldwyn and Beach),[28] he reluctantly visited Southern California; found it much to his liking and stayed, eventually founding the Hollywood Writers Club and serving as president of the Screen Playwrights, the American Writers Association, and the Authors' League of America. His *Patent Leather Kid* (First National) would be nominated for one of the first 1927–1928 Academy Awards category in writing of an original story. Another of his short stories would become

23. "Look Your Best Title Card," James O. Kemm Collection.

24. Hughes, *Souls for Sale* trailer, 16:12.

25. Brownlow, *Parade's Gone By*, 276.

26. Tibbetts, *Introduction to the Photoplay*, 138.

27. "Remembrance," 16, 21.

28. Hughes, "Early Days," 118.

the basis for Marie Dressler and W. C. Field's *Tillie and Gus* (Paramount, 1933).

Goldwyn's was a unique project, even allowing authors final powers of supervision over their pictures. Goldwyn sought great stories to match his stars, as he felt that screen stories had not advanced as rapidly as technology. "The industry rests upon solid bedrock of good stories and plays. Remove that and it will not stand."[29] According to Will Rogers, Hughes was "the original eminent author, and the only one who remained eminent after his first picture."[30] Honored not only with *Who's Who in the Theatre*, Hollywood saluted him as one of the wittiest toastmasters. Others praised him as one of the top contemporary 1929 American Playwrights.[31] Hughes was, without a doubt, a witty writer. Known for such inter-title aphorisms, as "her face was her chaperone," Rupert won a contest for the best front-page newspaper headline with his "POPE ELOPES!"[32]

As a writer, Hughes was also renowned for embedding (or tacking on) his ethical messages in his fiction. In many ways, he was morally a Victorian (and was once called the American Balzac), preaching duty, self-reliance, and respectability. He argued that religious stories and literature had a more terrible effect upon children's imaginations than the movies.

Biographer Kemm believed it "inevitable that Rupert would turn his attention as a novelist to the Hollywood colony he found so fascinating."[33] Earlier Hughes had written one of the earliest short stories about the movies: "In it a gang of thieves pretended to be a motion picture company

29. "Great Authors' Plans," 1480.

30. Kemm, *Rupert Hughes*, 190.

31. Burns, *American Playwrights of Today*, 246.

32. Kemm, *Rupert Hughes*, 316, 320.

33. Kemm, *Rupert Hughes*, 125.

and robbed a mansion while apparently using it for a scene of a story." Hughes had also written a vaudeville sketch entitled *Celluloid Sarah* about silent motion picture actors careless about their language. He juxtaposed what they were supposed to say with what they actually said. "Some of the dialogue was very ribald," Hughes confessed. "The hero, gazing adoringly at the heroine, might mutter, instead of the supposed sweet nothings: 'Move over, you thief; you're hogging all the space.' And his Juliet might answer with a languishing: 'Let me into the picture, you screen swine or I'll spit in your eye.'"[34] Having written humorous vaudeville sketches, he found the life of entertainment fascinating and recorded it with vividness. A gossip columnist for *The Bookman* called Hughes "as quick in his movements, as brilliant in arranging his always provocative sentences" as ever.[35] During the early days of the Depression, he penned *The City of Angels*, in which an ordinary lifeguard implausibly soars to film stardom.

In this novel, Hughes boldly announced, "If you are truly respectable, you never tell the truth about religion or marriage." He would be unrespectable, telling the truth as he saw it about both. Hollywood seemed more accepting than the Bible Belt, particularly regarding divorce laws. His own messy public separation from his first wife, Agnes, in 1904 led, in part, to his becoming a social crusader for divorce. Marriage often explodes when two peaceful chemicals are mixed wrongly. And, for Hughes, more liberal divorce laws only mean that "we are becoming more humane. And Hollywood is not the center of the divorce industry; Indiana, a farming state, is." When celebrating an old Hollywood couple whose marriage had lasted fifty years, Hughes preached that "Christ said nothing about a

34. Hughes, "Early Days of the Movies," 39.
35. "Sales for Soles," 493.

woman ever getting a divorce at all. He only allowed a man to get it on one ground. You cannot run this country by the church, especially while the churches do not agree on any one thing. Divorces are as popular and decent and as ancient as the world. Moses brought down from heaven the easiest system."[36]

His 1923 film *Reno* was, according to *Variety*, no more than "a lecture on divorce laws."[37] Critic H. W. Boyton of the *New York Evening Post* noted how Hughes took up such progressive social crusades as in his filmed theatrical drama *On Clipped Wings*, dealing with the marital toils and troubles of an actress, which essentially preached that the "moral conditions are no worse in the theatre than elsewhere."[38]

Hughes's overt moralizing frequently lambasted his readers by ironically referring to passages from their own sacred texts. A moving picture machine could have tempted Eve to "knowledge and started the eternal parade of wickedness" as much as the serpent. Flippant witticisms dot his text, where he quips that it is better "to smoke here than hereafter" or that "religious people flaunt their creeds, like actresses advertise their love." Crying about the absurdity of life to her mother, his heroine, Mem, cries out, "The Lord is another Charlie Chaplin, Mamma! He's just planted another kick where it will do the most harm." Mocking the backsliding doctrine of slow apostasy, Hughes indicates that Mem first opens the "forbidden closet by buying two fan magazines devoted to the moving pictures." (Hughes

36. Hughes, "Can't Blame the Movies," 2:20.

37. Kemm, *Rupert Hughes*, 72.

38. Boyton, "Hughes and His Work," cited in Kemm, *Rupert Hughes*, 72. Losing his second wife Adelaide to a tragic suicide in 1923 while she was traveling in China would provoke him further to denounce what he felt was religious oppression, in the publication of his controversial essay, "Am I an Atheist?," box 1:2.

does commandeer a classic line for his fictional producer Bermond, a thinly disguised Samuel Goldwyn, "the commercial demon, the fiend of sordid mercantile ideals." In the novel, Bermond tries to hire George Bernard Shaw as a writer, who retorts, "There is a hopeless difference between us, Mr. Bermond: you are interested in art; I am interested only in money.")

His early works contributed to the popularity of both Mary Pickford and Douglas Fairbanks, particularly with *Johanna Enlists* (1918) and a reworking of *Tess of the Storm Country* (1914/1922) for America's Sweetheart. Hughes took indirect credit for Fairbanks's success, as the actor had failed in one of Hughes's theatrical productions, *All For a Girl*. He spent time with Chaplin, marveling at the tragic Charles Lamb quality about the comedian, and claiming to have learned the mechanics of comedy and how not to crab (kill other people's laughs by moving) from the comedian.[39]

39. Hughes, "Early Days," 121.

5

THE NOVEL AS SERMON

S*ouls for Sale*'s heroine, Remember ("Mem") Steddon, exhibits "the appeal of a ripe peach." She is the attractive, obedient daughter of the Calverly town minister, the Reverend Doctor John Steddon, somewhere in Mark Twain country along the banks of the Mississippi. Reverend Steddon had not only never seen Los Angeles, but had never seen a moving picture, although he knew the world was going to wrack and ruin from the vile work of this vast, shapeless dragon, "the twentieth century's peculiar monster," the latest novelty of that odious Science that attacked religion, that Steddon sought to slay with his Savonarola-like denunciations. Yet, after hearing one of her father's sermons denouncing the evils of Hollywood, Remember muses: "I should like to see Los Angeles."

FIGURE 20

Reverend John Steddon rails against the evils of Hollywood
while his quiescent wife ignores his jeremiad
(courtesy *Silents Are Golden*).

In the novel, Remember is in love with Elwood Farn-
aby, the son of the town's most prominent drunkard (this
during the early days of Prohibition). Her father viewed
wedlock itself, however, as a solemnity, not a carnival; so,
inevitably in Hughes's gentle hands and purple prose, Remember becomes impregnated through a moment of innocent passion, religious ecstasy, and erotic intimacy. The two
choir members are "victims of the tidal wave" of lust one
Sabbath evening, after "a fervor of religious zeal and music
had exalted their emotions and made their hearts easy prey
to the moonlight." For Hughes, religious worship is as guilty
for evoking or inciting desire as the moving pictures. Then,
in the true formula of melodrama where the wages of sin
remain death, Elwood dies in a freak automobile accident
and Remember remains alone with her illicit secret.

Fearing exposure and scandal for her father and family, Remember heads to the southwest to bear her child and

begin a new life. Along the way, she suffers a miscarriage, takes on the role of a grieving widow, and meets some Hollywood film people, who draft her for a movie and compel her to come to Los Angeles. She becomes a popular melodramatic starlet and the scene is set for the battle of religion and movies. In all she does and is, Mem is an actress. She will become "another America's Sweetheart." The book chronicles Mem's fictional education into the liberating culture of Hollywood. Her travails will indirectly preach a sermon framed by the proposition: "The Bible never harmed anybody. But neither did the screen, really."

What the novel is mostly about, however, is Hughes's polemics against organized religion. Hollywood is the utopian alternative to a corrupt institution that has, according to Hughes, enslaved and duped millions. In the novel, Mem's struggles to get into the film industry are minor compared with her angst about breaking with her parents and her tradition. The thematic subtext is how can America leave behind its superannuated and effete religious traditions and find a new freedom and identity in the progressive state of California, or how can you keep a girl down on the farm or in the pews once she has seen the bright klieg lights of Hollywood?

Rupert Hughes painted the pagan cult of Hollywood with pleasant hues. Thursday nights are set aside for the "religious duty" of actors to attend Hollywood Hotel dances and to commune with the "laughing satyrs." Against the harsh and respectable realms of the East, here was Xanadu, where one ate California fruit "like Eve" or danced like Salome into receiving "half a kingdom" or at least finding someone to help you get ahead and maybe find you a job. Such analogies could be troubling to those who knew their Scriptures, but for most of the public, these were actual people out of the Bible whom Hughes included in his new sunshine garden.

Hughes came to the defense of his new religious home, becoming Hollywood's public relations expert, apologist, and secular preacher. Like poet Vachel Lindsay's rapturous eloquence waxing on the Photoplay of Religious Splendor as a form of "American hieroglyphics" or universal Esperanto, Hughes would take up the vanguard banner of a crusader.[1] His apologetics would include his fictional novel *Souls for Sale* as much as his essays. Ironically, the atheist Hughes celebrated one aspect of Christianity in Hollywood. Echoing publicist Laurence Sterne's commendation of religion in Hollywood, Hughes coauthored a tribute to the Reverend Neal Dodd of the renowned "Little Church around the Corner." For these authors, Dodd was the ideal churchman, a quiet High Church Episcopal priest praised for being a "sheep in sheep's clothing" and for bestowing his charity and concern for all sinners. Dodd's tireless work for the Motion Picture Relief Fund endeared him to the Hollywood community.

FIGURE 21

Bankers Laurance Hill and Silas Snyder published a public relations monograph to persuade religious readers of the goodness of Hollywood, almost parodying the question of Nathanael (John 1:46) about Christ himself (book cover photograph courtesy Darren Meggs).

1. Lindsay, *Progress and Poetry of the Movies*, 88–89.

The Novel as Sermon

What the authors point out is that at a time when ministers all over the country were hurtling anathemas at "the unspeakable sins of the modern Sodom and Gomorrah," Dodd built his little chapel; he was not a "superior prig" or "smugly virtuous exhibitionists" but a simple good progressive man of honesty. In his laud for Dodd, Hughes could not resist another diatribe against what he termed "the puritans and preachers of all denominations [who] assailed pictures as enemies of morality, corrupters of the young and the old, and wreckers of both church and home influences." They reviled people who made movies as heathen and a peculiar menace, "forgetting the sins they had bewailed in their own congregations and communities, the clergy almost as a unit rather implied that evils of every sort had probably been invented by the motion picture people and most certainly were enormously multiplied by their activities." Dodd, however, was like Father Damien, dwelling in the leper colony of Hollywood, but to Dodd, it was the City of Angels.[2]

Hughes became one of Hollywood's most active denizens. He would build a celebrated mansion along the lines of the Pickfair estate. He would publicize and defend his new homeland with all the passion of his art, and after seeing his first fig tree and eating of its fruit, would confess to feeling "Scriptural."[3] When his heroine leaves her provincial home town, she gets a liberal education on this "foreign world, another planet, where everything was unlike anything she had ever imagined." Coming into California is like coming up into a new Eden. Eventually she reaches the new Babel, which her father had denounced as the last capital of paganism. She thought that no city could be as wicked as she had thought Los Angeles would be.

2. Hughes and Wagner, *Two Decades*, n.p.
3. Hughes, "Early Days of the Movies," 121.

FIGURE 22

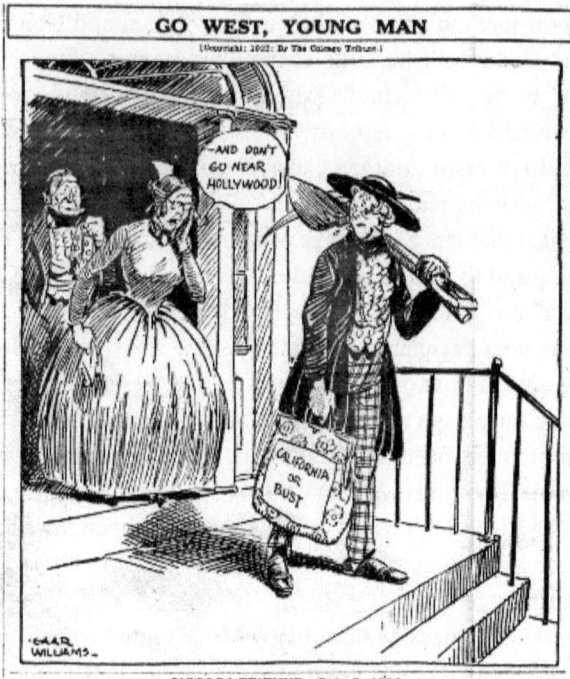

GO WEST, YOUNG MAN

[Copyright 1922: By The Chicago Tribune.]

—AND DON'T
GO NEAR
HOLLYWOOD!

CALIFORNIA
OR
BUST

CAAR
WILLIAMS

CHICAGO TRIBUNE   Feb. 8, 1922

Horace Greeley's advice notwithstanding, Middle America was wary
of the West Coast Babylon (public domain, courtesy Bruce Long,
Arizona State University).

The heroine's father speaks his jeremiads against this place "where orgies are held, a sin and a shame." For this fundamentalist preacher, the word Hollywood was "a synonym for riotous outlawry, a plague spot, a kind of spendthrift slums." Hughes counters this denunciation with his own public relations release: "However, the city which her father had damned with such wholesale horror, was ninetenths composed of mid-Westerners like him, people who had brought their churches and churchliness with them." For Remember, this new world would either prove ruination or celebrate redemption. In the wily hands of Hughes, the die was already cast.

Hollywood was, for Hughes, a sacred place. His novel would function as a sermon, extolling its virtues. In contrasting religion and the movies, he found more goodness among the movie people than among church people. Hollywood was a holy wood, as sacred a space as any camp meeting site and as holy as any sanctuary. Henry Wilcox who had planted the community with the intent of establishing an alcohol-free utopia had even given free land to the Presbyterians and others who would build churches.[4] In his novel, Hughes exhibits his habit of showing us the lovely estates of Hollywood, the places where Pickford, Fairbanks, and Betty Compson lived and made pictures and the long buildings where Harold Lloyd made family friendly movies.[5] Hollywood's holiness consisted in the fact that it maintained no legal Sabbath, but encouraged people whose "hearts felt as big and golden and juicy as their own oranges." It was a wholesome and uplifting place to live and work. However, Middle America imagined juicer, and more salacious, activity unfolding behind the orange groves façade.

4. Starr, *Inventing the Dream*, 3.
5. Lynd, *Middletown*, 266.

FIGURE 23

A Ralph Barton caricature of various Hollywood celebrities
appeared in "When the Five O'clock Whistle Blows in Hollywood"
in *Vanity Fair* (September 1921) with Buster Keaton and Rupert
Hughes in the center, Harold Lloyd and Will Rogers on the left
(public domain).

When Hughes's heroine goes "spooning" with her director to a secluded romantic spot up near Inceville Studio's moving picture fishing village, Hughes notes that this was the same canyon where Methodists held camp meetings and the paradise where the "Uplifters gave outdoor pageants." In fact, she experiences the "Enchantment of the *yuccas de Dios*, the tall white spikes of the candles of God"; although, it must be mentioned that the dim yuccas soon deteriorate into becoming "candles of a black Sabbath."

Ultimately, by looking at this alloy of actual and pretend worlds in film, "Mem felt she was getting a divine purview of the world. Life to her looked much what life must look like to God, where humanity must dance before Him as before her until each life was cut off or vanished in its final fade-out." When her mousy mother joins her in California, the beauties of California, "a land the Lord has been awful partial to," seduce her as well. Hughes sanctifies La-La-land and makes it holy ground.

FIGURE 24

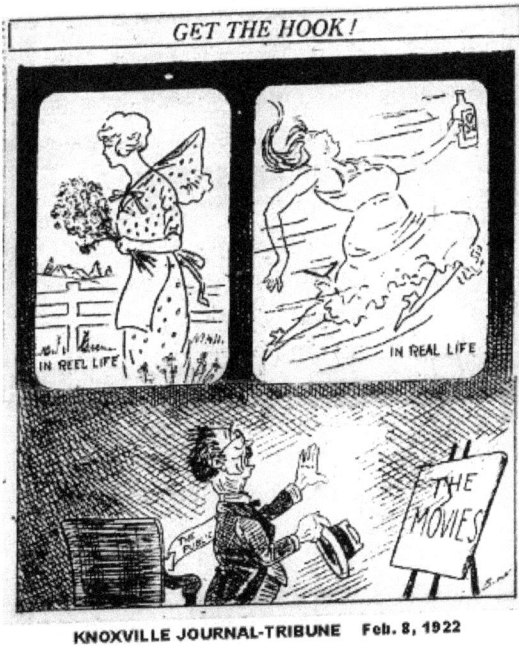

KNOXVILLE JOURNAL-TRIBUNE Feb. 8, 1922

Middle America suspected that behind the pristine and pure façade of Hollywood movies lay a lascivious lifestyle (public domain, courtesy Bruce Long, Arizona State University).

If Hollywood were Jerusalem for the new artists, then temples and synagogues speckled the American landscape, with one of the holiest sanctuaries being located in New York City, namely the sacred exhibition site of Roxy's Cathedral. When Mem goes to Broadway, she attends a theater every night and to a matinee every afternoon. "And she marveled that her father's religion had set the curse of denial upon the whole cloud realm of the drama. On Sundays, the theaters were closed except to 'sacred concerts,' but the good people who were trying to close the motion picture

65

houses had not yet succeeded." Mem and her mother also visit the Capitol Theatre, known as the supreme standard in motion picture exhibition, decorated with marble stairways, Etruscan gold, a grove of gilded trees and forests of columns as tall as the sequoias of California, fluted and capped in splendor, and illuminated with mural paintings by William Cotton. "Before the pictures was a Rothapfelian divertissement. A pipe organ roared its harmonious thunders abroad." Its sonorous tones were equivalent to calls to prayer as congregations prepared to see the sermons of the modern age. It was an electric church.

As early as 1909, University of Pennsylvania professor Simon Patten had noted the contrast of the old passing world and the new modern world separated by a few streets, with a crowd around the electric lights of nickelodeon and ice cream parlor, while on the other side, the church, library, and schools remain dark and closed.[6] A decade later, the *Christian Herald* photographed a similar scene of the two rival sites on a Sunday evening.[7] Hughes contrasts these two worlds of church and moviegoing: "One thing impressed Mem amazingly. She had just seen a handful of sleepy people at the once-a-week prayer meeting. Here she saw a packed movie house, the fifth packed house that day." Here she found vibrant and eager congregations who gathered freely to share in the silent, visual sermons of the day.

The defense of the art of the film also meant a defense against meddling moral reformers. Throughout his novel, Hughes marshals evidence against the impending

6. Patten, "Amusement as a Factor," 185.

7. "Two Pictures," 720. In contrasting the church and moving picture theater back in 1913, Vanderbilt University professor Carl Holliday quipped that the most peculiar difference between the two realms was that in the latter, "none fell asleep" ("Motion Picture and the Church," 353).

censorship of political and religious forces, chronicling the eternal battles between enforced morality and unencumbered liberty. Having closed the saloons with the Volstead Act, Hughes castigates "the busy agents of vicarious virtue" for closing moving picture houses on Sunday, clipping whole scenes out of films and subjecting them all to the whimsical approval of hired censors; he complains that they "assail tobacco as a devil's weed and forbid school-teachers to smoke even in their own homes." Mem's father unleashes his wrath against the movies as the weapons of Satan. Where the Puritans of Boston stripped Quaker women and lashed their bare backs for the good of their souls, so "the good Puritans of 1920 lashed the bare reputations of the moving-picture producers for the good of the community." Like novelist Nathaniel Hawthorne, whose relative had been the only unrepentant judge at the Salem Witch Trials, Hughes detested what he saw as a corrupt historical paradigm. When his heroine feels a pilloried public shame for "parking" with her director, she feels like Hester Prynne, fearing that guardian devils were floating about her.

Hughes's brand of Puritanism dictated the dualism of the novel. There were two kinds of people and places. Remember had been brought up as a Puritan to believe in duty first—in self-denial, abstention, modesty, simplicity, meekness, prayer, and remorse. In contrast, California people worshiped "the sun, flowers, dancing, speed, hilarity, laughter, and love. They despised the Puritans who abhorred them." Each saw the other as heathen or hypocrite, and Mem slowly adopts the view that the "most spotless exteriors are only whited sepulchers." A reformed theology gave way to an unabashed hedonism.

The charge of hypocrisy appears regularly in *Souls for Sale*. Mem writes her mother that "in Los Angeles I saw one of William de Mille's pictures where a pious Boer was reading from *The Songs of Solomon*, and when they quoted what he was reading, they had to blot out part of it on the title card. Think of that, mamma! Yet the Book is in every Christian home." Hughes complains that no censorship tampered the film production of Bible stories. He accuses the censors of closing their eyes to the prestigious Bible story pictures, and permitting "almost complete nudity and horrific crimes denied the secular films."[8]

In his novel, Hughes was generous enough to recognize the undercurrent of a religious film industry. He acknowledged that the "Methodists were doing something." The Methodist Episcopal Church had set up a film studio to produce pictures for use in Sunday schools and by missionaries and, by 1921, over four thousand Protestant churches had installed movie-viewing machines. The Methodists had even conducted their 1919 centenary in Columbus, Ohio, showcasing movie-making as a novel evangelistic idea, with a huge screen of 139' by 149' previewing hundreds of films for clergy. However positive these trends may have appeared, Hughes attacked what he called the wholesale reformers, or professional agitators who were lobbying for state censorship laws.[9] He believed that the Methodists' tactic of publishing "white lists," approving certain Hollywood films and condemning others, was a more subtle form of censorship.

Hughes's propagandistic asides poured oil on the fires of censorship then raging as he castigates the shame, tyranny, and asininity of censorship: he complained that films in Pennsylvania were more "prudish than a Sunday school library, as you couldn't refer to approaching maternity." Moving pictures, he wrote, should not be frightened, humiliated, or bullied. As an art, moving pictures should

8. Hughes, *Souls for Sale*, 383.
9. "Reformers Are Rapped," 1.

68

stand above the petty complaints of those philistines, because, for Hughes, the moving pictures combined all the arts of drama, fiction, landscape, sculpture, painting, psychology, philosophy, and a history of manners as much as Shakespeare's plays or Hudson River School artists like Jasper Francis Cropsey and Asher Durant. (Tom Mix films, for example, contain "landscape art of the noblest beauty.") Hughes recast his vision for moving pictures in religious terms: "You can call it art, merchandise, trash, wooden nutmegs, but you cannot rob it of its noble mission—to cast light into dark places." The celebration of created light, of the pronouncement "Let there be Light," connects this art to the genesis of creation, against any critical spirit of censorship.[10]

In defending Hollywood against the reformers, Hughes unleashed a multipronged attack on the church. He first accused churches of a Freudian projection, of making god in their own image, as Mem discovers that perhaps God's "poor, half-witted worshipers were endowing him with their own weak intellects, slandering him with their stupid reverence, and enforcing their own silly prejudices upon souls far wiser, though lacking the fearlessness of bigotry." Second, he argued that movies are not an "alibi for bad behaviors; whether little Willie goes out to hold up a train or your daughter elopes," you cannot, opined Hughes, attribute their moral delinquencies on the latest movie successes.[11]

Hughes's central point, repeatedly made, is that it would be ludicrous to "blame a twenty-year-old art for evils that had flourished during ten thousand years of recorded

10. Johnson, "Let There Be Light," 46.
11. Clark, "Can't Blame Movies," 1.

wickedness. The motion picture Goliath was felled by a shower of stones from the slings of myriad Davids."[12]

Believing that more clergymen populated penitentiaries than "their quota," Hughes compiled a list of over six thousand crimes by clergymen. He contrasted the unbalanced press coverage of the trial and acquittal of Arbuckle or of the kidnapping and murder of a young man by two young evolutionists, Richard Loeb and Nathan Leopold, "just for the thrill of it," with heinous crimes of ministers who had mistresses, committed murder, and did worse. He complained that no pulpit or paper would dare publish the appalling sins of the so-called righteous. "As for living the Christ life, it cannot be done, and it ought not to be done."[13] The narrative of his novel waxed eloquently, so much that it became a proselytizing sermon for a new religion.

12. For Hughes, "There were no movies twenty-five years ago, but Satan is a million years old, and he hasn't taken a day or night off yet" ("Can't Blame the Movies," 144). Hughes's studies of the Calvinist theology of the Puritans seemingly left traces of the doctrine of total depravity. Remember's friend Leva speaks for Hughes when she confides that: "I don't know a single moving picture person who is above reproach. But then, neither do I know a single person in any other walk of life who is above reproach. Everybody I ever heard of is full of sin. The Bible says that we all fell with Adam—and Eve. So I suppose it's only natural that movie people should be as faulty as everybody else is. But I can't see that they're any wickeder than anybody else."

13. Hughes, "Why I Quit," 23.

6

THE NOVEL RELIGION

H ughes slyly set up a subversive equivalence between church and movies. Not only was the clergyman's home "really a theatre," but his sermons were akin to dramatic fictions. Hughes would point out that, "*On Broadway* was to the actor what *in heaven* was to the saint."[1] Yet in his opinion, both professions told lies. "If certain people charge money for acting that means no more than the fact that most preachers charge money for preaching." His heroine had flown from her Egyptian captor, her father as the high priest of the old religion, with her sin, into the desert, where she

> found a new paradise, a new priest craft, a new religion beyond the desert. She had come to believe in an artist God, loving beauty and emotion and inspiring his true believers to proclaim his glories through the development and celebration of the fits and graces he had bestowed. She felt that he required of her hymns of passionate worship instead of the quenching of her spirit,

1. Hughes, *Souls for Sale*, 372.

the distortion of her graces, and the burial of her genius. The Mosaic Ten Commandments contained no "Thou shalt not commit dramaturgy." She felt a consecration, a call to act, to interpret humanity to humanity. What her father had deemed temptations and degradations she now considered inspirations and triumphs.

Hollywood stood for Hughes as a rival religion. His producer of comedy films, Mr. Rookes reveals "a priestly regard for his altars. A work of art was as solemn and as chaste a burnt offering to his god, the Public, as the oblation of any other priest before any other deity." It is his sacred duty to make people laugh. Hughes describes such a director as a "god in little. He could bid the rain rain, the wind roar, and the lightning blaze. He rode upon the storm he created."[2]

Directors and movies stars were the saints worshiped by millions. When the actor Holby approaches Mem with romance, she refuses his offer: "I don't want to be one of Solomon's wives. Half the women in the United States seem to claim you as their spiritual bridegroom. I would as soon marry a telephone booth or a census report. You make Brigham Young look like a confirmed bachelor." Hughes exposes a celebrity culture that has supplanted the devotion

2. Hughes does, however, allow one director, Claymore, to play the role of skeptic regarding "the parvenu priest-craft of the movies" (cited in Kemm, *Rupert Hughes*, 216); Claymore serves as a wary apologist for the movies, showing a critical loyalty to correct its faults "like he had done with his wife who left him on that account. He lovingly had chastised her. He wailed against the trash of the trade, its base commercialism. He was a Priest at the altar of movies, but he always praised the elder gods of the theatre" (249). Claymore talks to Mem frankly about her body and herself, as a sort of father confessor, "dissecting a soul before a believer's eyes"; he is Abelard to her Heloise, a spiritual tutor, "with teacher and student becoming involved in each other's souls, with a glimpse of their high spiritual relations" (238–39).

given to saints of old. "Medieval girls and spinsters set up images of saints and made violent love to them under the name of religion, clothing amorous raptures in pious phrases, and burning with desires that they interpreted as heavenly longings." Now the photographs of actors transform into holy icons on walls or bureaus, and Mem becomes one of them, put on a shrine and worshiped.

When she becomes an actress, the gods of Hollywood bestow upon her one of their most marvelous gifts: she is imbued with the gift of communication, able to speak "language that men of every nation understood." Mem "was speaking this long-sought Esperanto for everybody to understand." When he was filming *Intolerance* (1916), D. W. Griffith scolded his young actress Lillian Gish for calling the movies "flickers." He remonstrated that the Bible predicted this glorious new "God-given" medium with its "universal language" to "repair the ruins of Babel," and when brought to its full power, moving pictures could end wars and usher in "the millennium."[3] Hughes recycles a similar sentiment when his heroine wonders why movies were greeted with such hostility, contempt, and fear. "She did not understand that they who teach the world a new language or open a new world, or bring golden gifts to any sort to the people are always crucified at first by the Pharisees. Later their converts become Pharisees for new Messiahs." The word is made celluloid and all people are drawn to it. In a mixed message, Hughes charts the evolution of the moving pictures from the early days of "one-eyed booths" into "cathedrals where thousands would gather" daily. Hollywood was now a "Cinematic Tower of Babel," which for him was a good thing. It enabled men and women to speak a universal language.[4]

3. Gish, *Lillian Gish*, 358.
4. Brownlow, "Lillian Gish," 22.

FIGURE 25

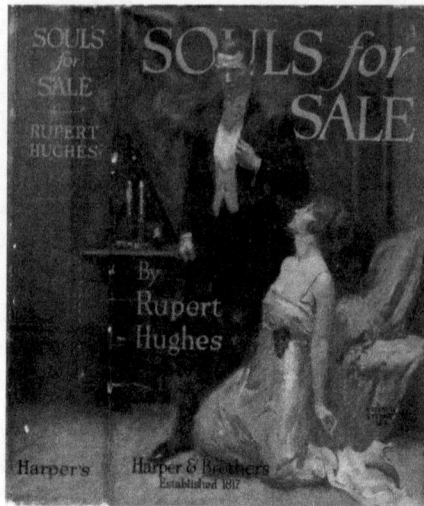

The provocative cover of the 1922 novel titillates with Mem at the feet of her Hollywood director (public domain).

Mem's first pictures were "going about the world like missionaries winning proselytes to her shrine." Near the end of his novel, she reflects on her new calling:

> What better things could anybody learn in a church than here, mamma? Aren't God's gifts developed? Isn't he praised in color and music and sermon and sympathy? It's all hymns to me—hymns of light and sound, sacred dances and travel into the noblest scenes god ever made.
>
> Yet they call it a sin even to go there, and they say there is a bill coming up to close all the theaters as well as the barber shops and delicatessens on Sunday, so as to drive the people to church or force them to stay at home in dullness—poor souls that work all week and don't want to got to dull church and sleep before a dull

preacher. They don't want to be preached at: they want to be entertained?

According to them I'm a lost soul on my way to hell. Yet my heart tells me that I'm leading a far, far, far more worshipful life building pictures than I ever could have done back there in Calverly, if I'd stayed there and been good and married a good man and gone nowhere but to church and the kitchen and the nursery all my days.

And look at that biblical picture to-night! I saw the one before with Adam and Eve—both stark naked except for a few bushes. They'd have put the actress in jail if she had played like that in anything but a Bible story. If religion can sanctify a thing, why can't art?

They give prizes to little girls to read the Bible through from cover to cover. Even papa praises that as a soul-saving thing! He made me read it all, and it includes the Songs of Solomon and a hundred stories that leave nothing horrible untold.[5]

Near the end of the novel, Mem looks upon her father's church as a grave. She had brought resurrection to life through her positive gifts of acting. In particular, she felt her home and church had been nearly devoid of laughter and mirth, "except of an infantile, ecclesiastical sort. Her father had been one of those who could never think of Christ as wearing any smile but one of pity of forgiveness. A laughing messiah was incredible, horrible." So, she attends the service of one of the great gods of the moving pictures, Charlie Chaplin, and finds her gaiety in his work of "the noblest quality, rich in pathos as in hilarity," namely Chaplin's recently released *The Kid* (First National, 1921). Hughes inserts that as Abraham Lincoln leaned on Artemus Ward

5. Hughes, *Souls for Sale*, 382.

to help him through difficult times, so now "Lloyd George begged for a comedy of Charles." Remember is transformed from a morose to cheery disposition through the movies, finding a laughing god of Nietzsche's in the little tramp. Attending the comedy makes her "a new person. She is changed, because going to a farce was like going to a school of the highest educational value." It is the message of the movies, not of the church, that transforms one's life.

Meanwhile, back at home, in old melodramatic style, the old mortgage of the church is overdue; foreclosure is imminent. The "manager of the motion-picture house here offered to share the profits on the showing of a picture in which, as he had the impudence to tell me, my daughter played a part." Such an act for the father would be collaborating with evil, and he "put Satan behind me." Nevertheless, movie money given clandestinely enables the church to survive, evidence from Hughes that the film industry can perform another spurious miracle.

FIGURE 26

For Hughes, as for H. F. Hoffman's cartoon, the hypocrisy of the clergy occurred when they could see profits in using movies in church ("The Sermon / The Business Meeting," *The Moving Picture World* 7 [1910] 202; courtesy Library of Congress).

The Novel Religion

It is not enough that the daughter leaves home and discovers her hope in the moving pictures, but Hughes must reconcile all humanity under the banner of the movies. When her father welcomes back Remember, he espies his daughter as a "sumptuous Delilah floating." He marvels at how "ungodly beautiful" she is and prays in a parody of the devout Simeon's prayer (*Nunc dimittis*) in Luke 2:29, "I thank Thee, O God! Now lettest Thou Thy servant depart in peace." While Mem begs his forgiveness for all the heartaches she had caused him, he is the one who is converted.

Back in her old village, a crowd gathers at the movie theatre, the Calverly Capitol. "From *that* sanctuary she greeted her old Sunday school teacher." At the dinner table, the old preacher's humble grace for the bounty of the Lord saddened Mem again. He, who had suffered every hardship, was grateful for bounty.

Mem adopts a supralapsarian doctrine of evil: "If I hadn't been a fallen woman I couldn't have saved papa's church from ruin." After Mem sees *The Beggar's Opera*, "the wickedest thing I ever did see," she realizes that "if it hadn't been for that, Handel wouldn't have written 'The Messiah.'" She went on with diabolical logic, indulging in a parallel providence, "If Eve hadn't eaten the apple, then Christ would never have come to earth." Out of sin comes triumph, she thought, and if she had not sinned with Elwood, the church could not have been rescued. Inspired by Thomas Jefferson's notion that "when great evils happen, I am in the habit of looking out for what good may arise from them as consolations to us; and Providence has in fact so established the order of things as that most evils are the means of producing some good."

Father Steddon finally goes with his daughter to the movies. In a scene reminiscent of Methodist minister Hartwell Spencer's autobiographical *One Foot in Heaven*, where a father is converted to the good morality of the movies by watching a William S. Hart movie, so another transformation occurs: "'Where my daughter goes is good enough for me!' He chuckles. 'Then, my beloved wife and daughter, I want to plead for the forgiveness of you both. I have been wrong headed and stiff necked as so often, but now I am humbled before you in sit of all my pride. It has just come over me that when God said, "Let there be light," and there was light, he must have had in mind this glorious instrument for portraying the wonders of his handiwork.'"

The reconciliation between father and daughter brings the story to its own paradise, echoing the moral lesson that historian Tom Gunning interpreted in Griffith's *The Drunkards' Reformation* (Biograph, 1909), namely that the dramatic arts transform lives and restore the Victorian home.[6] Reverend Steddon humbly acknowledges his mistake: "Our dear Redeemer used the parable for his divine lessons and it has come to me that if he should walk the earth again today he would use the motion picture. My daughter you are using the gifts that heaven sent you as heaven meant you to use them. Your eloquence is far greater than mine has ever been. Never have I seen the beauty of purity amid temptation so vividly brought home." The art of the movies is sacred. It will ennoble humanity.[7] Mem's response to her father's turnabout is to kneel by her old bed and "on knees unaccustomed to prayer, implored strength to keep her gift like a chalice, a grail of holiness. She woke with an early morning resolved to be the purest woman and the devoutest artist that ever lived."

6. Gunning, "From the Opium Den," 30.

7. Such an insight of the movies as parables was articulated a decade before in 1911, when Congregational minister Herbert Jump published his pamphlet, *The Religious Possibilities of the Motion Picture* (South Congregational Church, 1911).

7

THE BOWDLERIZED ADAPTATION

Serialized as a *Redbook* magazine series, Harper and Brothers published *Souls for Sale* in 1922. The novel reviews acclaimed it as "atrocious."[1] Even Hughes did a dyslexic parody outline of it in 1923 for *The Bookman* entitled "Sails for Soles."[2] If the novel had been read more, it might have proved more controversial and blasphemous. As it was, it slipped into oblivion until eminent author Hughes decided to film it. However, as a film, it did not rise too highly above its source; critics deemed it as passable. But the movie adaptation did fare better in reaching an audience, even if being consigned to the status of pure twaddle. "Speak to most exhibitors about *Souls for Sale*," opined the *New York Times* reviewer, "and they will grin, tell you it is hokum, and add that it's something that appeals to their audiences."[3]

The film differs radically from the book. As a photoplay, *Souls for Sale* offers that adolescent fantasy that one

1. Behlmer and Thomas, *Hollywood's Hollywood*, 119–20.

2. "Sales for Soles," 601.

3. "Review: *Souls for Sale*," 2.

could go to Hollywood and become a star overnight. Unlike the book, the comic melodrama eschews most of the religious issues that Hughes preached and focuses on the plight of an ordinary girl who makes good in the film industry, showing the various bits of glamour, adventure, and romance that one connects to the city of dreams. All of this is embellished with real stars and studio locations as a sort of "a personally conducted trip behind the scenes of movieland." According to the *New York Times* review of the film, the story that traces Remember's journey from nobody to stardom is "false and trivial"; nevertheless, Hughes's ability to show the inner workings of the make-believe filmland made the whole enterprise fascinating. As one film reviewer for *Photoplay* put it, "The action is loose, the story reeks with heavy villainy, and the acting is never impressive—but the background of studio life puts it over."[4]

After Goldwyn Pictures' *ars gratia artis* opening trademark, the movie abruptly begins with Remember Steddon (Eleanor Boardman) recently married to Owen Scudder (Lew Cody), transformed from the novel's tragic and innocent young lover into a notorious murdering polygamist who has supposedly tricked Mem into this suspicious bond. She sits on the porch of a train caboose speeding through the desert to Los Angeles with her new husband. As Scudder touches her hand, she realizes with an exaggerated revulsion and terror, that she is the bride of this strange, creepy man. When the train stops for water, she leaps off and scurries into the dark. She wanders into her wilderness, stumbles upon a deserted cross among the sage-filled dunes, and faints. Her pose parallels the famous magic lantern stereopticon slide of the Toplady hymn, *Rock of Ages*, in which a maiden clings desperately to the wooden cross.

4. Smith, "Review," 65.

The Bowdlerized Adaptation

Hughes parodies the classic Magic Lantern slide of *Rock of Ages*, transporting his sinner to the desert with his shot of Mem not quite clinging to a cross in the desert (courtesy Joseph Boggs Beale Magic Lantern Slide and Screenshot, Stu Minnis).

In a cutaway shot, we see her father, the Reverend John Steddon, practicing his next Sunday's sermon before his absent-minded wife. With closed fist and pointed finger, he fulminates, "O Hollywood! Hollywood! Thou movie-mammon that leadest our children astray, and teachest them wickedness! O Los Angeles, thy name should be *Los Diaboles*." While Mother looks wistfully upon the loving photo of their daughter who has been seemingly been carried off to China by this man Scudder, the Father prays, "God bless her and guide her wherever she goes."

Staggering under the heat of the burning sun, her help comes from the hills as an actor, Tom Holby (Frank Mayo), the handsome western star dressed as an Arab sheik riding a camel finds her, picks her up, and cradles her in his arm. Her first question to him is one that drives to the heart of the reality of Hollywood image as much as to the authenticity of the Christian faith, which Hughes disparages.

> "Are you real or a mirage?" She asks him.
> "Neither," he responds, "I'm a movie actor." He asks, "Are you better now, Miss . . . ahem?"

"Remember Stedden," she answers.
"Oh, I always will," he puns.

FIGURE 29

**Saved by a sheik of the burning sands, Mem (Eleanor Boardman)
goes from the Bible Belt into Hollywood stardom
(courtesy Silents Are Golden).**

The sheik, a self-reflexive industry joke on actor Rudolph Valentino, gives the languished runaway a canteen of water from which to drink, reviving her. A title card explains, "The usual sheik led the usual captive across the usual desert." When the director Frank Claymore (Richard Dix) comes to find his wandering actor, he finds him hunched over Remember and exclaims, "Good Lord, Tom Holby, is there anywhere in the world where you don't find a fan?" To which Holby responds forlornly, "She's no fan; she never heard of me." As each of the rivals take turns holding and nursing her, the competition for the milk-fed maiden begins, setting up the fantasy for all young wannabes heading to Hollywood. Within several years, the casting couch would take on notorious connotations. In his *Mirrors of Hollywood*, published in 1925, Charles Donald Fox acknowledges the allure of Hollywood for Midwestern girls. "Lives there a girl with a soul so dead who never to herself hath said, 'I, too, can act upon the screen!' Such a naïve maiden is forewarned: 'TELL YOUR FRIENDS: Don't try to *Break into the Movies* in Hollywood Until You Have obtained FULL, FRANK AND DEPENDABLE IN-FORMATION From the HOLLYWOOD CHAMBER OF COMMERCE. IT MAY SAVE DISAPPOINTMENTS!'"[5] Movie moguls, from Goldwyn to Louis B. Mayer, preyed upon the ambition of young girls since the early days of Hollywood, seeking trysts in turn for opportunities, most of which never materialized.

FIGURE 30

WICHITA EAGLE   Feb. 11, 1922

The prevailing public image of Hollywood in the early 1920s, with the Arbuckle scandal, envisioned a life of debauchery and exploitation (public domain).

5. Fox, *Mirrors of Hollywood*, 55, 61.

FIGURE 31

IT'S AN ILL WIND, ETC.

RIVERSIDE PRESS Feb. 17, 1922

While newspapers thought scandals in Hollywood would deter young women, legions still poured into the City of Dreams (public domain, courtesy Bruce Long, Arizona State University).

Hughes downplays these casting room scenes in the film. In a desperate move, Mem connives tries to get a job through the director, Claymore (Roy Atwell), whose office overflows with beautiful women. An intertitle explains his plight, as he "has about two jobs a day to give out and endures more wiles than King Solomon." Mem had heard that the only way to succeed in the movies is to sell your soul. She had nothing else left to sell. She watches one vamp, Velma Slade (Eve Southern), touch the casting director's arm, bat her eyes, and grab him. He indicates he will be with her in a moment. Slade tries to seduce him and indicates that she is willing to "pay the price." The remarkably honorable and gallant director admonishes Slade who "had nothing left to sell," except her soul. He tells her (and all the young wanna-bees in the movie houses), "You poor simp! Selling yourself to me would not sell you to the director or the producer. It's the public you've got to sell yourself to—not to us!" Watching the travesty, Mem realizes that "souls were a drug on the market." The lesson Hughes sets forth is that more often than not, the filmmakers are of noble stock. In fact, when Hughes "daringly" shoots a famous Hollywood Hotel party where "many of the famous movie stars dance there until the heathenish hour of eleven thirty, unless they are too tired to keep awake so long," he couches the potential scandal with having numerous movie mothers chaperone the young people. The propaganda that promotes more of a decent movie community than a Hollywood exposé continues unabashedly. What makes Hollywood an even more assuring sanctuary is this ubiquitous presence of "movie mothers," acting as chaperones or dreaded dueñas.

FIGURE 32

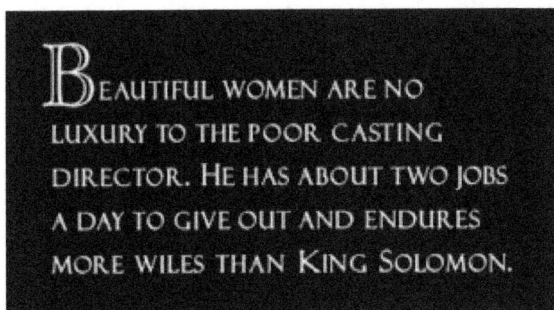

BEAUTIFUL WOMEN ARE NO LUXURY TO THE POOR CASTING DIRECTOR. HE HAS ABOUT TWO JOBS A DAY TO GIVE OUT AND ENDURES MORE WILES THAN KING SOLOMON.

Hughes's intertitle altered the public perception (and perhaps reality) of casting directors as dutiful servants of a noble art (Courtesy Silents Are Golden).

Mem is given a screen test, dressed up as a beautiful captive harem girl, under so much grease paint that her own mother would not recognize her. She makes her way to Hollywood to seek employment. Its appeal of glamour lures her westward. Hughes lays out another point in his sermon through an intertitle: "Hollywood, ridiculously abused and caricatured, seemed to Mem a paradise of homes and gardens and mountain vistas of the sea." White hillside stucco bungalows and palm trees decorate the screen, painting an idyllic setting of a good life.

What follows next is a sheer commercial for the film industry even as Mem trudges afoot, pleading vainly for an opportunity at the Famous Players Lasky, the Metro, and the Fox Studios. Over twenty-five famous stars dot the landscape of Hollywood as well, giving what one reviewer noted as a "very fair idea of motion picture life in Hollywood." Dressed in informal clothes, Charlie Chaplin directs a scene from his *A Woman of Paris* (1923), lying on the lawn to get the right shot and smoking incessantly (apparently, opined one review, in a great hurry to go on a fishing trip to Catalina Island). Chaplin vainly tries to direct her riding a horse, laying on the ground to capture her in a low angle, putting cigarettes into his mouth and then tossing them without lighting any. In another behind-the-scenes glimpse, Mem visits Erich von Stroheim's set of his infamously long *Greed* (1924), as he oversees Jean Herscholt, with music playing for atmosphere. A young intense Stroheim models Herscholt on how to comb his hair and chew a cigar, as violins and cello play music to sway the actors' mood.

FIGURE 33

Providing a cameo for Hughes's movie about moviemaking,
Charlie Chaplin directs on the set of his *A Woman of Paris* (1923)
(courtesy Stu Minnis).

She becomes one of five hundred anonymous extras in a mob scene in a bow-tied and knickered director Fred Niblo's *The Famous Mrs. Fair* (1923), where she gets to wave a handkerchief from a window in an extremely long shot. At the stock company commissary lunchroom, she encounters such luminaries as Chester Conklin, Kathryn Williams, and June Mathis. She watches T. Roy Barnes teasing Zasu Pitts, but falling off his bar stool. One of the effects of such cameo appearances was to show scores of Hollywood people "seated at the democratic tables of the studio restaurant, proving that they eat their meals with the same enjoyment as people in other lines of business." It was the art of demystifying the scandalous Hollywood crowd as just ordinary people.[6]

6. "Review: *Souls for Sale*," 14.

Claymore hires her for his new film *Chivalry*, an apt title for so principled a man. He tries to make her into a comedienne, giving her a costume and an acting test. When his lead actor Hobly starts putting the movies on Mem, Claymore asks what's going on. Holby responds, "What's it to you?" Claymore retorts, "None of your damned business," suggesting Clark Gable's Rhett Butler's language had precedent. The exchange will become a running gag throughout the film.

Given an opportunity to be comic, she fails miserably and weeps when the screen test is projected. Director Claymore tells her, "If you could only cry that well on camera." Of course, she can. He also gives her advice to be natural and not make faces: "Don't try to act funny. Just *feel* funny. The camera photographs exactly what you are thinking of." He then helpfully promises her: "I'll make an actress of you if I have to break your heart and every bone in your body." The promise does not sound that comforting.

In one ironic scene, Claymore puts Mem behind prison bars and an intertitle caustically proclaims that there "aren't as many actors in jail." Hughes obliquely alludes to his own editorials where he harangued about the multitude of religious people in prisons. Hughes goes on to preach that "when an actor gets into trouble, they blame the screen. A scandal is fatal to anyone in the moving pictures." No subtlety here. Mem is playfully warned to beware of scandals. Hughes expertly works in the notion of her surreptitious marriage (and a possible divorce) with a photograph of her "husband" displayed as a wanted poster on the jail office wall. Here is Mem's hidden scandal, "an unfortunate marriage."

Nevertheless, Mem's roles become increasingly worthwhile. She appears in a society drama, dressed and festooned with feathered hats and long elegant gowns, as if playing in a glamorous DeMille costume set piece. Romantic intrigue continues with the director and leading man, with the former ordering the actor to "leave that nice little girl alone." Holby answers, "What's that to you?" Claymore now responds, "None of your damned business." In the production of a special circus life spectacle, lights fall on the lead actress, who must be replaced. Claymore takes Mem aside and lectures her, in what would become a standard Hollywood trope, "You'll have to take her place. [She] got her chance the same way." Mem jumps in and her career climbs to dizzying heights.

FIGURE 34

In an extravagant allusion to the costume dramas of Cecil B. DeMille, Hughes poses his stars on an elaborate staircase (courtesy Library of Congress).

Returning to the real drama of the family, Mem has not told her parents what she is doing, knowing how her father adamantly opposes their sinful corruption. Mem never "dreamed that her fame had already reached her home town"; however, the gospel of Hollywood goes back to the Midwest as it goes around the world. Her parents come to visit her in Southern California and discover her performing a trapeze act with Holby. They gasp seeing the actors on high wires and when they fall, they almost faint. However, seeing them land on a net, her father runs to hug her, but the mug that turns around is a male stunt double in a wig. Her parents embrace her, but try to cover her skimpy outfit. All she asks of them after this long-separated reunion is, "Promise me solemnly that you won't tell anyone here I am married." They looked stunned and can only say, "We came to take you home, and none too soon."

Holby introduces himself as a potential son-in-law and Clayborne praises their daughter as "an actress to be proud of!" Hughes adds an intertitle, "As Oliver Herford said to Bishop Potter: 'Actresses will happen in the best regulated families,'" a reference to an old story about the reassurance offered by humorist and cartoonist Herford (known as the witty Dorothy Parker of his day) when the bishop's nephew married the young actress Cora Urquhart.[7]

However, the baffled father goes defeated back to his pulpit, while the pampering mother stays with Mem. This marks the end of the religious commentary by the film, shortchanging the polemics of the novel, but protecting what it thought might be a larger audience revenue. But alas, the movie becomes even more unbearably ponderous. While some have thought that Hughes must have been being ironic, the continual reiteration of the American values of diligence and hard work become mere sermon points.

7. Bayard, "Fun I've Had," 169.

For example, Hughes includes an intertitle extolling the virtues of the Hollywood workforce, not at all ironic:

> However gorgeous or troubled, the movie folk must rise early and work late and factory hard. . . . To make their faces and bodies and souls interesting to the workaday world that buys them by the yards, the toilers of the screen endure every hardship, every hazard, night and day.

Meanwhile, her undisclosed husband continues his own wicked adventures, lining up his next spinster victim and robbing her of her bank savings. He escapes to Cairo, where with his next prospective prey, Lady Jane, attends a cinema showing. Watching the film, he spies Remember, in the jail scene. He sits in the balcony engrossed in her performance among a crowd of smoking Egyptians, who read subtitle cards in French and Arabic. Ironically, his date, Lady Jane, dupes him. He heads back to California to blackmail his original quarry, Mem.

The story switches to the avaricious and murderous motives of Scudder. Seeing photographs of Mem's two suitors, he compares himself in a mirror to them and then smashes the two photos together. Confronting a surprised Mem in her villa, he approaches her like a campy Nosferatu, asking where his wedding ring was. When she confesses that she threw it away after discovering that he was a beast and a murderer wanted by the law, he grabs her throat and declares his love. He wants the money and her salary that pays for her pearls.

When she responds, "They're not real," he cruelly poses, "Is there anything about you that is real? You actress!"

FIGURE 35

HARTFORD COURANT   Feb. 21, 1922

Ironically, the shadow of the Taylor murder haunts the murderous
character of Scudder in *Souls for Sale* (public domain, courtesy
Bruce Long, Arizona State University).

Then, she responds in lines that reveal how the Hollywood religion has begun to shape her very soul: "The
money I slave for is real. A scandal would ruin me."

Playing more like a devil's advocate, he charges her
with hypocrisy: "Your dear public wants to be fooled into
believing you as innocent as the parts you play." He then
mouths a line that Hughes has used against the institution
of marriage, barking that she belongs to him. And with
Hughes's libertarian assertion of selfhood, she counters, "I
don't belong to anybody. I belong to myself."

Rescued temporarily by her suitor, Claymore proposes
a strange marriage of mutual materialism: "I can't offer you
much except hard work and the privilege of being torn to

pieces by the critics. But I will build your soul to its height and sell it to the world if you let me."

Mem gets her big break in an early circus version of *A Star Is Born*, when the lead actress breaks her leg. Just as Mem ascends the height of her neophyte career, her villainous husband appears. During the final night of shooting, the director worries that a California hurricane (which is a miraculously rare event even with the Santa Ana winds at their worst) "threatens to overtake his artificial storm, carrying the circus 'tent to hell' and turn our picture into a tragedy."[8] The show must go on. In fact, director Claymore resolves to finish the picture with the impending storm, putting Mem on a fractious horse and telling the cameramen to keep shooting, no matter what happens.

Lightning strikes the circus tent, plunging the entire set into darkness. A yellow-tinted fire breaks out and extras panic. Of course, the cameramen are told to keep grinding. Like a bad scene out of *Day of the Locust*, sets collapse, flames consume the big top, and the mob runs amok. Even with the rain, fire, wind, and catastrophes escalating, the cameras keep rolling. Simultaneously, the murderous husband Scudder sneaks around like a snarling beast, brandishing a gun. The director seeks to capture this thug. He declines to contact the police due to the possibility of a newspaper scandal.

The power plant that supplied the electricity for the nighttime lighting is struck by lightning (that God would intervene with such force is an unintended irony) and the circus is plunged into darkness with hundreds of extras panicking, fainting, going berserk. A wind machine's propellers threatens to slice anyone to pieces. As the hurricane

8. Such a cataclysmic ending hinted at the types of apocalypse preached by premillennialists, fueled by the dispensationalism of the *Scofield Reference Bible* commentary that would destroy the present evil age.

continues, Mem is knocked off her horse; trapeze artists fall without nets, and the cameras keep rolling. An injured actress asks for a mirror, "Give me a mirror. I've played my last part." In the midst of the storm, chaos, conflagration, and threats of Scudder, the director orders his cameramen a third time to keep cranking the cameras no matter what happens.

As the crew works to save the menagerie, Scudder tries to destroy one of his rivals, Holby, by driving a wind machine at him. When Mem runs blindly toward the wind machine propeller that would cut her to pieces, Scudder intercedes, throwing down his life to save her. At the last moment, in his unexpectedly strange conversion, Scudder confesses to Mem, "I was never right, head nor heart. I did one thing right. You were never my wife." The transformation of the thief on the cross is a simple conversion compared to Scudder's unmotivated change of heart.

With Scudder's dead body lying on the ground, the expedient director, "evidently always keen on his work," asks Remember to do the scene "just once more." Director Claymore wins Mem and arranges the last scene for a final fade-out in the fiery embers of the circus tent. The director tells his crew, "I've thought up a scheme for a final fade-out with the fire in the back ground." He tells his rival Holby, "As long as it's only acting, Tom, you may put a little more love into the scene." He embraces Mem, but the director cuts in and replaces Tom as the stand-in who gets to kiss her.

Hughes ends his cinematic sermon with one last bit of pathos, lecturing his audience of the true nature of Hollywood's community: "They are only players, after all; but they mean well and work hard, spinning pictures for the amusement of strangers. And they can never know, until it is too late to change, whether their toil will win them censure or applause."

The crisis between her sweet Victorian home and the corruptions of Hollywood appear reduced to a few cutaways of her father, the Reverend John Steddon, who practices his Sunday sermons by pounding his fists in the air and mouthing the one line against Hollywood in the entire picture: "O Hollywood! Hollywood! Thou movie-mammon that leadest our children astray, and teachest them wickedness! O Los Angeles, thy name should be Los Diaboles!" When her parents arrive to visit her in Hollywood, they are mistaken for extras. They believe they see her fall from a trapeze swing and her mother faints, but then they discover that their daughter's double fell into a net. Nevertheless, for them, while Hollywood remains a madhouse, they are happily reunited with their daughter with no hint of religious tension. They even agree to continue the deception of not letting the studio know that Mem is married. The baffled father returns home to his pulpit quite content with his daughter's success.

FIGURE 36

Hughes emphasizes the film's happy ending, as Mem gets to stay in Hollywood while her reverend father returns to the Bible Belt (courtesy Stu Minnis).

Two months after the release of the film, the *New York Times* showcased the author as one who translated his words into images: "A few authors, most prominent among them, Mr. RUPERT HUGHES, now not only write but direct their own pictures. Mr. HUGHES is perhaps not the greatest of living artists, but his pictures are better than the average, and their defects are the defects of his imagination and not of his knowledge."[9] However, in his work on the best motion pictures of the era, critic Robert Sherwood called the film "propaganda" and an "exposé of conditions in the citadel of cinema," but one that paled in comparison to James Cruze's 1923 film, *Hollywood*.[10]

9. "Motion Picture Arts," 10.

10. Sherwood, *Best Motion Pictures*, xix, 84.

CONCLUSION

THE FAUSTIAN BARGAIN

> The production is called *Souls for Sale* for one thing, because it was the title of the original story when it appeared in a magazine, and also because it smacks of wickedness. But there is nothing wicked in "Souls for Sale" except the villain, who has to be, and he saves a life before he dies.[1]

Playing off Goethe's story of *Faust*, Hughes teases his audience with a titillating title. The notion of selling one's soul generally sparks a stereotypic expectation such as actor Tom Holby "selling his soul to the devil" for money and fame, amid a "Babylonian horde of scarlet women." The general perception of Hollywood in the early 1920s was that if movie-making were an industry, the selling of the merchandise of dreams, so were souls to be viewed as "commodities, merchandise like ships or shoes or sealing wax, to be traded on the market." Mem at one point hears the kind of "hellish laughter as Faust's Gretchen heard."[2]

But for Hughes, what was destroying the fabric of the American soul was religion, not the movies. "It is baffling

1. Sherwood, *Best Motion Pictures*, 84.
2. Hughes, *Souls for Sale*, 76.

to find that nothing is more effective in destroying certain souls than the attempt to save them." Hughes opts for the modern American capitalist way, arguing that it is better to sell one's soul for success than to give it away.

Rupert Hughes's controversial novel made its small dent in Hollywood. Author and filmmaker, citizen and historian, atheist and patriot, Hughes wrote a narrative that incorporated his basic beliefs and his vision of a new world promulgated by a new medium. His transition from his famed writing into being a celebrity director, however, had not started auspiciously. In fact, on his early directorial attempts, classic film historian Terry Ramsay opined that as a "stellar writer of fiction for the *Red Book* magazine," Rupert Hughes "flopped with his first lavish scenario of Mr. Ziegfeld's *Gloria's Romance*."[3] Critic for *Photoplay*, Frederick James Smith, found little to praise about Hughes's melodrama. Mostly, he thought, *Souls for Sale* offered a peek behind the screen and a trip through Hollywood,

> a Cook's Tour of the empire of celluloids. As such, it will fascinate those who have longed to visit a studio in operation—and, we suspect their name is legion. It is for this reason that *Souls for Sale* lands among our chosen six. The story behind this journey through Filmland is false and trivial, tracing a young woman from extra to stardom. But, when Hughes places his camera behind the camera and shows how make-believe becomes apparently real, then *Souls for Sale* has high interest. The action is loose, the story reeks with heavy villainy, and the acting is never impressive—but the background of studio life puts it over.[4]

3. Ramsaye, *Million and One Nights*, 703.
4. Smith, "Review," 65.

Conclusion

A *Variety* critic discerned Hughes's motive, believing that the film was the biggest thing by Hughes as screenwriter and director. "It is also a remarkable piece of propaganda for Hollywood, the picture industry as a whole, and its clean-living acting people as well."[5] However, in the end, the film enjoyed only a short-lived public enthusiasm, with slim and dwindling crowds. Hughes mused that this was because people expected the film to be an exposé of "the terrific wickedness of the modern Gomorrah." Then when they "found instead a story emphasizing the hard lives of the toilers and the merely human and normal procedures of their love affairs, they warned their friends to stay away."[6]

Reflecting in 1935 upon the early days in the movies, Hughes scripted a two-part article for the *Saturday Evening Post*. His opening lines harkens back to the theme inherent in *Souls for Sale*, where he confesses to denouncing (tongue-in-cheek) Thomas A. Edison as "the devil incarnate and redivivus; for it was Edison who had fathered the motion picture and brought the knowledge of sin into the Eden that existed before its invasion into the world."[7] The novel punctuates this idea with exclamation points; the movie downplays the religious controversy or tension.

5. "Review 1947: *Souls for Sale*," *Variety*, May 16, 1947, 3.

6. Hughes, "Rupert Hughes at Home."

7. Hughes, "Early Days," 18.

FIGURE 37

Rupert Hughes Directing a Scene From Inside the Fireplace in "Remembrance." (Based on The Saturday Evening Post Story, "Pop")

Before directing *Souls for Sale*, Rupert Hughes portrayed a grateful daughter in his sentimental drama *Remembrance* (1922) (courtesy Library of Congress).

Mem becomes an allegory for Hughes's vision of recent womanhood. She had dwelt in "puritanical respectability as in a kind of mental harem, with a yashmak on her demure mind and shapeless black robe of modesty over her bundle some clothes." But now, she sheds her past, leaves the dark ages of ritual, and joins a "vast hegira of humanity into a new era of all things good in their place. Her soul and her body were her own now." She learns that a pretty woman is merchandise and that she could sell herself for the sake of the world. "She had wares for the market of movie making and could barter for fame and future."[8]

---

8. At the end, she leaves her town "no longer a scapegoat, sin laden, limping into the wilderness, but a missionary, God-sped into the farthest lands of the earth." And she leads her little sister "out of the dark into the light of Hollywood" (404). Mem is the one who atones for the sins of the father and religion by sanctifying entertainment.

Conclusion

In contrast to the happy romantic travelogue of the film, the novel recommends that small town girls escape the confines of the Bible Belt and go west to find not only fame and fortune, but themselves as well. However, what followed were more cautionary tales, especially in light of the Arbuckle scandal and its fuller political impact. With yellow journalism spreading a toxic wave of ignominy throughout Hollywood, the industry did become, according to critic Robert Sherwood, a Ninevah, Tyre, Babylon, Sodom, and Gomorrah. "It was the subject of many an ardent sermon," he noted, and consequently it became "a Mecca for tourists."[9]

While Will Hays would appear as a moral czar and guardian, Hollywood had now become tainted with the poisonous sewage of the scandals. Its disgraced image would endure, fester, and become responsible for all the ills of society, in spite of Hughes's early protestations to the contrary. Even if Hollywood hadn't invented sin, it surely sold it for profit at the cost of its soul.

Like the treatment given his hero Charlie Chaplin, society publicly vilified Hughes and marginalized him as a notorious anti-religionist; however, ironically, he proved himself a zealous conservative, ardently championing American civil religion, passionately preaching US preparedness during World War I, and later proclaiming his adamant opposition to fascism and communism. In December 1941, he would proudly publish, "I am an American" in *The American*, just as Pearl Harbor was attacked. Eventually, his rabid patriotism would lead to his conversion to aggressive conservative politics and collaboration with HUAC against the Hollywood Ten. He fought the fellow travelers of the American Authors Authority, whom

---

9. Sherwood, *Best Motion Pictures*, 84.

he claimed endangered both property and souls.[10] In May 1947, *Variety* would report that eminent author Rupert Hughes testified that the Screen Writers Guild was "lousy with Communists."[11]

The irony of Hughes's optimistic modernist ideology culminates in a Presbyterian doctrine in the depravity of human nature. The early celebration of the "goodness of man" could not endure. *Deus ex machina*, without the Deus, constructs a contrived plot point where *Souls for Sale* is suddenly resolved through an unlikely occurrence. Scudder's sudden repentance before hitting the propellers of a gigantic wind machine seems a bit manufactured, so artificial that not even Hughes could believe it. But then the entire narrative is a comedy, even though in Goldwyn's words, "Our comedies are not to be laughed at."

That Mem is a "respectable minister's daughter" who marries a serial killer would raise sufficient number of eyebrows, but that ingenuous, albeit stupid, decision, helps to camouflage her descent into the dens of iniquity of Hollywood. Like an adept magician, Hughes creates sympathy for his wayward heroine by focusing attention on the immoral villain. Reviewing the film decades later, critic Roger Ebert pointed back to the Fatty Arbuckle scandal of 1921, seeing the film as Hughes and Goldwyn's "exploitation of the national fascination with Hollywood and its transgressions."[12]

What the movie does most effectively is announce that modernity has arrived. The father minister has gone home to the Bible Belt; the mother is sidelined. Perhaps the greatest ideological change is that of Mem, who speaks the new dogma of Hollywood, to her sleazy husband. "Scandal

---

10. Kemm, *Rupert Hughes*, 288.

11. "Review 1947," 3.

12. Ebert, "Review."

will ruin me." Sin is no longer an enemy; it is only a public relations nightmare.

Historian Susan Craig observed that liberal theology,

> with its themes of universal salvation, its acceptance of a pluralistic polity and, above all, its emphasis on divine immanence, was general enough to appeal to a wide range of Christian and Jewish believers. Even those whose skepticism had driven them from the churches probably found these messages, devoid as they were of evangelical proselytizing, harmless enough to merit no more than mild lampooning in the critical press.[13]

A notorious novel *Souls for Sale* adapted for the screen actually became harmless. Significantly, Remember's only friend and confessor, and the rational and modern substitute voice of the author himself, is the town doctor Bretherick, who had tried to write stories for the movies and has a savvy creativity that enables Remember to rewrite her life: "I'm one of those pernickety authors that believe that actresses should act and let authors auth." The doctor's gift, like that of the creative writer, was knowing how to "lie." "He did not believe in Doctor Steddon's creeds. They were cruel legends in his opinion. He pictures preachers as men who slander the beauties of this world in order to glorify a false heaven of their own concoction." Both preaching and acting were, for Hughes, arts of deception, with moviemaking possessing the more honest and fascinating fictional muse.

In adapting the novel to film and seeking to appeal to a larger market, Hughes erased its religious satire, marginalizing any theological significance. Perhaps under the sway of Goldwyn's famous quip that if he wanted to send

13. Craig, *Skin and Redemption*, 197–98.

a message, he'd call Western Union, Hughes downplayed what was incendiary in his original text. The film's erstwhile celebration of Hollywood's core values, even if done so ironically at times, set about a modernist hegemony of money, fashion, celebrity, and status. The worship of Mammon replaced a Victorian morality in the film, with the realization of the necessity of selling one's soul to the world. Hollywood and America would worship its new progressive religion, at least until the stock market crash and the emergence of an ecumenical partnership of Protestants and Roman Catholics under the leadership of Joseph Breen to clean up the industry during the Depression. And while *Souls for Sale* would slip into oblivion, it had been successful in trading its soul and a bowl of porridge for fame and fortune. After all, didn't the Bible say, "God helps those who help themselves?" Well, maybe not, but Franklin's words sound promising.

FIGURE 38

The narrative trajectory of Hughes's satire on faith and filmmaking mapped out the entire film (courtesy Tim Lussier, Silents Are Golden).

BIBLIOGRAPHY

"Afraid of Billy Sunday." *Variety*, November 17, 1916.

Anderson, Milton. *The Modern Goliath*. Los Angeles: David, 1935.

Behlmer, Rudy, and Tony Thomas. *Hollywood's Hollywood*. New York: Citadel, 1975.

Berg, A. Scott. *Goldwyn*. New York: Knopf, 1989.

Berle, Milton. *Milton Berle: An Autobiography*. New York: Delacorte, 1974.

Bierce, Ambrose. *Collected Works*. London: Forgotten, 2011.

———. *The Devil's Dictionary*. New York: Pauper, 1958.

Billings, M. E. *Crimes of Preachers in the United States and Canada*. San Diego: Truth Seeker, 1914.

Bogdanovich, Peter. *Allan Dwan: The Last Pioneer*. Westport, CT: Praeger, 1971.

Brownlow, Kevin. "Lillian Gish." *American Film* 9 (March 1984) 22.

———. *The Parade's Gone By . . .* Berkeley: University of California Press, 1976.

Burns, Mantle. *American Playwrights of Today*. New York: Dodd, Mead, 1929.

Butler, Jon, et al. *Religion in American Life*. New York: Oxford University Press, 2000.

"Church to Give Shows as Aid to Spiritual Teaching." *Variety*, April 8, 1921, 1.

Clark, Doris. "Can't Blame Movies for Your Shortcomings: Rupert Hughes." *San Francisco Daily News*, August 15, 1922, 1.

Claussen, Dane S., ed. *Sex, Religion, Media*. Boulder: Rowman and Littlefield, 2002.

Cocks, Orrin G. "Studies in Social Christianity: Motion Pictures." *Homiletic Review* (1916) 217–23.

Cooper, James. *Knights of the Brush: The Hudson River School and the Moral Landscape*. Manchester, VT: Hudson Hills, 1999.

Bibliography

Craig, Susan. "Skin and Redemption: Theology in Silent Films, 1902 to 1927." PhD diss., CUNY Academic Works, 2010.

De Courssey, Forbes. "What about the Morals of Hollywood." In *Can Anything Good Come Out of Hollywood?*, by Laurance Hill and Silas Snyder, 31–33. Hollywood: Snyder, 1923.

Dorrien, Gary. *The Making of American Liberal Theology: Idealism, Realism and Modernity, 1900–1950*. Louisville: Westminster John Knox, 2003.

Ebert, Roger. "Review: *Souls for Sale*." *RogerEbert.com,* July 29, 2009. https://www.rogerebert.com/reviews/souls-for-sale-1923.

Ellis, William T. *Billy Sunday: The Man and His Message*. Philadelphia: Winston, 1914.

Emerson, John, and Anita Loos. *How to Write Photo-Plays*. New York: McCann, 1920.

"Eminent Authors Pictures Formed." *Moving Picture World*, June 7, 1919, 1469.

"Fairbanks Heads 'Non-Sense' Film Ridiculing Censorship: Rupert Hughes in Propaganda Picture." *Variety*, April 15, 1921, 44.

Ferre, John P. *A Social Gospel for Millions: The Religious Bestsellers of Charles Sheldon, Charles Gordon, and Harold Bell Wright*. Bowling Green, OH: Bowling Green University Popular Press, 1988.

Fox, Charles Donald. *Mirrors of Hollywood*. Hollywood: Renard, 1925.

Gish, Lillian. *Lillian Gish: The Movies, Mr. Griffith and Me*. With Ann Pinchot. Upper Saddle River, NJ: Prentice Hall, 1969.

"God Helps Poor Girls—Says Billy Sunday." *Virginian-Pilot*, March 19, 1922, 19.

Goldbeck, Willis. "Mr. Hughes and the Photodrama." *Motion Picture* magazine (1922).

Grant, Percy Stickney. "If Christ Went to the Movies." *Photoplay* 17 (1920) 29–30, 121.

"Great Authors' Plans Are Outlined." *Moving Picture World*, June 7, 1919, 1480.

Gudreault, Andre, and Tom Gunning, eds. *Une Invention du Diable? Cinema des Premiers Temps et Religion*. Sainte-Foy, Quebec: Les Presses de l'Université Laval, 1992.

Hill, Laurance, and Silas Snyder. *Can Anything Good Come Out of Hollywood?* Hollywood: Snyder, 1923.

Holliday, Carl. "The Motion Picture and the Church." *Independent* 74 (1913) 353–56.

Horton, T. C. "Cleveland Moffett's Crazy Quilt." *King's Business* X: 5 (1919) 395–96.

"Hughes." *Los Angeles Times*, January 10, 1950, 2.

Bibliography

Hughes, Laurence A. *The Truth about the Movies by the Stars.* Hollywood: Hollywood, 1924.

Hughes, Rupert. "Are You a Humanist?" *Humanist* (1951).

———. "The Art of the Moving Picture Composition." *Arts and Decoration* (1923) 9–10, 79–80, 91–92.

———. "Can't Blame the Movies for Your Shortcomings." Rupert Hughes Papers, USC Libraries Special Collections Box 017: Box 2, Folder 20.

———. "Early Days in the Movies: Part II." *Saturday Evening Post* (1935) 118, 121–22.

———. "The Necessity for Originality in Photo-Plays." In *The Truth about the Movies by the Stars,* by Laurence A. Hughes, 373. Hollywood: Hollywood, 1924.

———. "Rupert Hughes at Home in Hollywood." *New York Times,* June 9, 1923, 10; *New York Times,* January 15, 1923, 18.

———. *Souls for Sale.* New York: Harper, 1922.

———. *Souls for Sale* trailer. Carl Van Doren Letters, Box 16, Folder 12, Princeton University Archives.

———. "Why I Quit Going to Church." *Cosmopolitan,* October 1924.

Hughes, Rupert, and Rob Wagner. *Two Decades: The Story of a Man of God, Hollywood's Own Padre.* Los Angeles: Young and McCallister, 1936.

Hutchison, William R. *The Modernist Impulse in American Protestantism.* Durham: Duke University Press, 1992.

Ingersoll, Robert. *The Gods and Other Lectures.* Washington, DC: Farrell, 1892.

———. *Liberty of Man, Woman and Child.* N.p., 1877.

Johnson, Julian. "Let There Be Light!" *Photoplay* 16 (1919) 46–48.

Jump, Herbert A. *The Religious Possibilities of the Motion Picture.* In *The Silents of God,* by Terry Lindvall, 54–78. Lanham, MD: Scarecrow, 2001.

Kaestle, Carl, et al. "The History of Readers." In *Literacy in the United States: Readers and Reading Since 1880,* edited by Carl F. Kaestle et al., 33–74. New Haven: Yale University Press, 1991.

Kemm, James. "The Literary Legacy of Rupert Hughes." *Books at Iowa* 42 (1985) 10–25.

———. *Rupert Hughes: A Hollywood Legend.* Beverly Hills: Pomegranate, 1997.

Kinkead, Joyce. "The Western Sermons of Harold Bell Wright." *Journal of American Culture* 7 (1984) 85.

Langman, Larry. *A Guide to Silent Westerns.* Westport, CT: Greenwood, 1992.

Bibliography

Lindsey, Vachel. *The Art of the Moving Picture*. New York: Liveright, 1970.

———. *The Progress and Poetry of the Movies*. Edited by by Myron Lounsbury. Lanham, MD: Scarecrow, 1995.

Lindvall, Terry. "God in the Saddle: Silent Western Films as Protestant Sermons." *Australian Religious Studies Review* 21 (2009) 318–44.

———. "The Organ in the Sanctuary: Silent Film and Paradigmatic Images of a Suspect Clergy." In *Sex, Religion and Media*, edited by Dane Claussen, 108. Boulder: Rowman and Littlefield, 2002.

———. *Sanctuary Cinema: The Origins of the Christian Film Industry*. New York: New York University Press, 2007.

———. *The Silents of God: Selected Issues and Documents*. Lanham, MD: Scarecrow, 2001.

———. "Sundays in Norfolk: Toward a Protestant Utopia through Film Exhibition in Norfolk, Virginia, 1910–1920." In *Going to the Movies: Hollywood and the Social Experience of Cinema*, edited by Melvyn Stokes, 76–93. Exeter: University of Exeter Press, 2008.

Longworth, Karina. *Seduction: Sex, Lies, and Stardom in Howard Hughes's Hollywood*. New York: HarperCollins, 2018.

Lopez, Kathryn Jean. "Writing Mencken." Interview with Terry Teachout National Review. https://www.encyclopedia.com/arts/educational-magazines/teachout-terry-1956.

Lynd, Robert S., and Helen Merrell Lynd. *Middletown: A Study in Modern American Culture*. New York: Harcourt Brace Jovanovich, 1929.

Marsden, George M. *Fundamentalism and American Culture: The Shaping of Twentieth Century Evangelicalism, 1870–1925*. New York: Oxford University Press, 1980.

Marty, Martin E. *Modern American Religion 2: The Noise of Conflict, 1919–1941*. Chicago: University of Chicago Press, 1991.

May, Lary. *Screening Out the Past*. Chicago: University of Chicago Press, 1980.

McConoughey, Edward M. "Motion Pictures in Religious and Educational Work." *New York Federal Council of the Churches of Christ in America*, 1916.

Morgan, David. *Protestants and Pictures: Religion, Visual Culture, and the Age of American Mass Production*. New York: Oxford University Press, 1999.

———. *Visual Piety: A History and Theory of Popular Religious Images*. Los Angeles: University of California Press, 1998.

"Motion Picture Arts." *New York Times*, June 9, 1923, 10.

"The Motion Picture as a 'Handmaiden of Religion.'" *Literary Digest* 64 (May 1920).

Bibliography

"Movie-Making an Art." *New York Times* 8, May 13, 1923, 3.

"Movie Men Favor a Federal Censor." *New York Times*, February 1922, 1.

Nord, David. *Faith in Reading: Religious Publishing and the Birth of Mass Media in America*. New York: Oxford University Press, 2004.

Overton, Grant. *An American Night's Entertainment*. New York: Appleton, 1923.

Palmer, Frederick. *Photoplay Plot Encyclopedia*. Hollywood: Palmer Photoplay, 1922.

Patten, Simon. "Amusement as a Factor in Man's Spiritual Uplift." *Current Literature: Religion and Ethics* 467 (1909) 185–88.

Potamianos, George, and Kathryn Fuller. *Beyond the Bowery: Cinema and Mass Entertainment in Small-Town America from Its Origins through the Multiplex*. Berkeley: University of California Press, 2008.

Ramsaye, Terry. *A Million and One Nights*. New York: Simon and Schuster, 1926.

"*The Re-creation of Brian Kent*: Ad." *Christian Advocate*, October 2, 1919, 1272.

"Reformers Are Rapped at Meeting: Movie Men Decry Activities of Professionals." *San Francisco Daily News*, August 15, 1922, 1.

Reiser, Andrew Chamberlain. *The Chautauqua Moment: Protestants, Progressives, and the Culture of Modern Liberalism, 1874–1920*. New York: Columbia University Press, 2003.

"Remembrance." *New York Times* 7, October 1, 1922, 3, 21.

"Reverend Billy Sunday Says." *Virginian-Pilot*, September 30, 1917.

"Review: *Souls for Sale*." *New York Times* 7, June 17, 1923, 2.

"Review 1947: *Souls for Sale*." *Variety*, May 16, 1947, 3.

Romanowski, William D. *Reforming Hollywood: How American Protestants Fought for Freedom at the Movies*. New York: Oxford University Press, 2012.

"Rupert Hughes." *Variety*, April 18, 1921.

"Sales for Soles." *Bookman*, June 1923, 441, 493–94.

Sheldon, Charles M. *In His Steps: Special Photoplay Edition*. [Victoria?]: Burt, n.d.

———. "In His Steps Today: What Would Jesus Do with the Drama?" *Christian Herald*, December 4, 1920, 1247–48.

———. "The Use and Abuse of Fiction." *Independent*, April 24, 1902.

Sherwood, Robert E. *The Best Moving Pictures of 1922–23*. Boston: Small, Maynard, 1923.

The Sins of Hollywood. N.p.: Hollywood, 1922.

Smith, Frederick James. "Review." *Photoplay* 24 (1923) 65.

Bibliography

Smith, Gary S. "Charles M. Sheldon's *In His Steps*." *Fides et Historia* 22 (1990) 47–69.

"*Souls for Sale*." *New York Times*, June 26, 1922, 16.

"*Souls for Sale*." *New York Time*, April 9, 1923, 14.

Staiger, Janet. "Conclusions and New Beginnings." In *Une Invention du Diable? Cinema des Premiers Temps et Religion*, edited by Andre Gudreault and Tom Gunning, 353–60. Sainte-Foy, Quebec: Les Presses de l'Universite Laval, 1992.

Starr, Kevin. *Inventing the Dream: California through the Progressive Era*. New York: Oxford University Press, 1986.

Stockton, E. Boudinot. "The Picture in the Pulpit." *Moving Picture World*, October 26, 1912, 336; November 16, 1912, 642–43; December 21, 1912, 983.

Stokes, Melvyn, ed. *Going to the Movies: Hollywood and the Social Experience of Cinema*. Exeter: University of Exeter Press, 2008.

Stowe, Harriet Beecher. *My Wife and I; or, Harry Henderson's History*. New York: Ford, 1872.

Tibbetts, John, ed. *Introduction to the Photoplay*. Shawnee Mission, KS: National Film Society 1977.

Trollinger, William Vance, Jr., ed. *Literacy in the United States: Readers and Reading Since 1880*. New Haven: Yale University Press, 1991.

"Two Pictures." *Christian Herald*, October 14, 1922, 720.

Veiller, Bayard. *The Fun I've Had*. New York: Reynal and Hitchcock, 1941.

Whissel, Kristen. *Picturing American Modernity: Traffic, Technology, and the Silent Cinema*. Durham: Duke University Press, 2008.

Wilkins, Thurmin. *Harold Bell Wright DAB Supplement*. Washington DC: Library of Congress, 1973.

"Words from Wise in Washington Make Censorship Problem Clear." *Variety*, April 8, 1921, 47.

Wright, Lord William. *Motion Picture News* 21 (1912) 14.

www.ingramcontent.com/pod-product-compliance
Lightning Source LLC
Chambersburg PA
CBHW032234080426
42735CB00008B/851